BUSINESS MANAGEMENT FOR THE WORKING MUSICIAN

A STEP-BY-STEP GUIDE TO

MAKING MONEY MAKING MUSIC

JOHN E. LAWRENCE

Copyright © 2018 by John E. Lawrence

All rights reserved.

ISBN: 97809995739-3-8

Edited and Published by

Detroit Ink Publishing

Detroit MI

http://detroitinkpublishing.com/

Cover Drawings by

John E. Lawrence

Ypsilanti MI

Cover Design by

Sydnee Turner of Sydgrafix

Detroit MI

http://sydgrafix.com

No part of this book may be reproduced in any form or by any electronic or mechanical means, including information storage and retrieval systems, without written permission from the author, except for the use of brief quotations in a book review.

Printed in the U.S.A.

About the Author

John E. Lawrence is a world-renowned guitarist and musician and the retired Director of the Washtenaw Community College (WCC) music performance program. A music instructor at WCC for almost 40 years, John was also the founder and producer of the school's *Living Legends* series, which brought famous musical acts such as *The Temptations, Mavis Staples, The Four Tops,* and *Ashford and Simpson* to the college.

John is a professional musician, a recording artist, an author, and an artist. John has recorded six CDs and written three instructional guitar books for Mel Bay™ publications.

TABLE OF CONTENTS

Chapter 1 1

Building a career doing what you love to do 1

The Definition of Work 1

Two ways to approach work 2

Negative Views of Artists and Musicians 4

POSITIVE VIEWS OF ARTISTS AND MUSICIANS 6

Follow Your Dream 8

Reasons Why People Are Not Successful 8

Playing It Safe and Taking Risks 10

Chapter 2 11

Choosing an Occupation 11

Assessing your talents and skills 13

Make a list of things that you enjoy doing 13

Things to Consider Before You Start Giving Private Lessons 16

Make Your Own Flowchart 22

Chapter 3 23

Putting Your Band Together 23

Every Band Needs a Leader 24

How to Maximize Your Rehearsal Time 26

Performing with a Music Sequencer 28

Chapter 4 31
Assessing Your Band's Worth 31

Chapter 5 38
How to Get a Gig 38

Preparing a Bio 38

The Four Tops 40

Ashford and Simpson 42

John E. Lawrence Bio 49

Designing Your Business Card 52

Making Your Contacts 53

Putting on a Musical Showcase 54

How to Keep a Gig 54

Finding the Right Gig 55

Working with a Booking Agency 56

Things You Should Know About Playing Clubs 59

The More Music You Know the More Often You Can Work 60

How to Put Together a Show 61

The Truth About Why Some Musicians Cannot Find Work 61

Musician Michael Moore: Bio and Advice 65

Things Every Musician Should Know 67

Chapter 6 70

Contacting Record Companies 70

Putting Together a Letter of Introduction 70

Sample Letter of Introduction 70

Creating a Demo CD 71

Chapter 7 74

John E. Lawrence's Steps to Success 74

Finish What You Start 76

About Washtenaw Community College (WCC) 79

Who's Behind The Program? 80

Developing a Winner's Attitude 81

Changing Your Habits 83

Excuses Are for Losers 83

Do Not Have a Victim's Mentality 84

Take Responsibility for Where You Are in Life 84

Examining the Seven Leadership Qualities 84

Chapter 8 86

How to Generate Interest from the Press 86

Writing a Press Release 86

Important Media Tips from Janet Hawkins 88

Letting the Right People Know That You are There 92

Putting Together a Press Kit 92

Create a Media List 93

Promotion: How and When to Promote 94

Posters, Flyers, and TV 94

Create a Mailing List 95

The Market Analysis 96

Chapter 9 99

Utilizing the Internet 99

YouTube 100

My Space 100

Twitter 100

Chapter 10 101

Putting Together a Practical Business Plan 101

Establishing Multiple Sources of Income 102

From Being an Employee to Being an Employer 103

View Yourself as a Business 105

Self-employment and Why It is the Best Job Security 108

Making Money During Hard Economic Times 109

Chapter 11 110

The Five Most Expensive Addictions 111

Choosing the Right Mate 113

Chapter 12 115

The Importance of Establishing Good Credit *115*

Avoid the Credit Card Trap *115*

How to Get Out of Credit Card Debt *116*

Keep Good Tax Records *117*

Working Corporate Engagements *118*

Being a Professional On and Off the Stage *118*

Chapter 13 ....**120**

Developing and Producing a Product *120*

Different Professional Branches *121*

Advice from Graphic Designer Michael Tanner *122*

CDs Recorded and Produced by John E. Lawrence *125*

How I Landed a Book Publishing Deal with Mel Bay Publications *134*

Chapter 14 ....**143**

Turning Points in My Life *143*

A Support System and the Importance of Positive Reinforcement *144*

Chapter 15 ....**149**

Personal Growth *149*

Preface

Let me begin by saying I am a professional guitarist with forty-six years of experience. During this time, I have learned some things that have enabled me to earn a living and I have been doing so for over 35 years. You may have heard stories about the starving artist as well as stories about the superstar entertainers that have earned millions, but did you know that there is a middle ground for artists that most people don't know about; a middle ground that enables an artist to earn an income that ranges from $50,000-$300,000 per year. This is an income that most people in the workforce earn. Occupations range from factory workers, engineers, attorneys, doctors, teachers, small business owners and many more. If earning this type of income is fine for those professions, then why would it not be good enough for a musician?

I can honestly say that I love my work. I actually look forward to going to work and I have to tear myself away from it in order to do my daily activities. How many people do you know that can honestly make that statement? On a musician's income, I have been able to acquire homes, automobiles, and recording equipment to build a recording studio, a guitar collection and a home fitness facility. I could go on, but I believe that I have made my point.

Someone once said, "If you love the work you do, you will never have to work a day in your life." As the rest of the world may say such familiar phrases as, "(TGIF) "Thank God it's Friday" or "Living for the Weekend", this would not apply when a person loves what they do for a living. Most jobs pay every week, bi-weekly or in some cases, once a month. As an artist, you can earn a good living, receiving a paycheck as often as you want and have a good time doing it.

There is an everyday occurrence that most people have to deal with at the beginning and end of their workday; I'm talking about rush-hour traffic. Most people have to deal with the daily hustle and bustle of rushing to and from their jobs. In some cases, jobs they may not like. Let's think about that for a moment. The average person spends most of their week doing something they may not enjoy. That is an awful lot of time devoted to doing something you may not enjoy and being someplace you may not want to be.

When you consider that there are twenty-four hours in a day, eight of which are spent working, another eight is spent sleeping, that only leaves you with eight hours to live life the way you want. If you include drive time back and forth to work, you can cut those eight hours down to six hours when you factor in rush-hour traffic. It is no wonder that people are so uptight. I believe there is a direct correlation between people who are unhappy in the work force and road rage. People who are unhappy with their lives tend to take it out on other people.

Introduction

This book will teach artists to market their skills as a musician. It will also instruct students on interpersonal skills, preparing a portfolio, booking performances, preparation and analyzing contracts, and negotiating skills to determine a monetary value for a musician's work. Students will learn how to manage their business while creating a multi-faceted career. Careers include musician, entertainer, engineer, arranger, producer, instructor, publisher, author, manager, and booking agent.

OBJECTIVE: To help you to assess your skills and potential to decide what careers to pursue. This book will explore money making opportunities via multiple occupations in the music industry. It will also prepare students to seek out job opportunities as well as promote the benefits of being an entrepreneur.

This book is not written from a manager's or booking agent's point of view; someone who does not directly earn money from being a musician. It is written from the perspective of a Virtuoso Guitarist that has earned a living primarily as a musician for the past thirty-five years. This book will explore the skills and lessons learned from that experience, which include survival skills, life skills, organizational skills, business principles and professional etiquette. It will also provide practical and logical solutions for applying them as they relate to a living artist.

I am someone that loves music and understands what it takes to work towards becoming the best musician that you can be. I have put in eight to eighteen hours a day practicing my instrument, and now at the age of fifty-five, I feel a need to practice more. This is because I have accepted the responsibility of being the kind of musician that other artists can learn from. I have accepted the responsibility to exemplify the kind of musician that displays excellence, creativity and style in their music. It is for this reason that I wrote this book.

In order to make a living as an artist you must believe in yourself, have courage, and have a sense of urgency. You must practice your craft and study often because self-doubt will set in if you have not done the necessary preparation that will enable you to do the job.

Courage without proper preparation brings discouragement, which will prevent you from getting anywhere. It will prevent you from attaining the financial success that is needed to sustain your career. A sense of urgency without courage brings frustration. Therefore, in order to be successful as an artist you must possess the following three traits:

(1) Belief in yourself - The dictionary defines belief as acceptance of truth of something. Acceptance by the mind that something is true or real often underpinned by an emotional or spiritual sense of certainty.

(2) Courage -The dictionary defines courage as the quality of being brave. The ability to face danger, difficulty, uncertainty or pain without being overcome by fear or being deflected from a chosen course of action.

(3) A sense of urgency - The dictionary defines urgency as, importance, necessity, or need. The need to deal with something quickly. The feeling of wanting something very much or immediately.

This book is written with the assumption that you either have the skills and knowledge to carry out the job or are in the process of acquiring those skills. When you are ready, this book will navigate you through the challenges that an artist faces while establishing a career. It will also aid in creating plans and strategies for building a solid foundation for earning a living in the arts.

Although this book was written from a musician's perspective, it can be applied to any form of the arts.

CHAPTER 1

BUILDING A CAREER DOING WHAT YOU LOVE TO DO

Most people choose their occupation based on job availability and salary. They then pursue the necessary education in order to make the job a reality. Whether the education comes from an institution of higher learning, trade school or on-the-job training, they complete the required work to move into a particular field. When the time is right, they join the workforce and start earning their living. Unfortunately, more often than not, they realize after landing the job, they really don't enjoy performing that type of work. They neglected to ask themselves one important question, what type of work would I really enjoy doing?

Now they have to make a choice! Do they go back to school and start all over again? Do they move into a different line of work? Do they settle for the job they have? After all, they are making a good income, the job has good benefits, job security, and room for advancement. Most people would settle for keeping the job they have.

How is it that so many people end up with jobs they do not like? One answer could be when people think of the definition of work, they look at it from the perspective of a noun. Let us examine some definitions of the word "work" as noted in the Encarta Dictionary: English (North America).

THE DEFINITION OF WORK

Work (noun)

- paid job - paid employment at a job
- duties of job - duties or activities that are part of a job or occupation
- someone's place of employment - the place where a person is employed
- time spent at place of employment - the time someone spends carrying out his

or her job

Work (verb)

- to have a job - to have a paid job
- to exert effort - to exert physical or mental effort in order to do, make, or accomplish something, or make something do this
- to function - to function or operate, or make something do this
- to be successful - to be effective or to achieve the desired result
- to exert influence - to produce results or to exert an influence

TWO WAYS TO APPROACH WORK

When "work" is looked at as a noun, it is a place that you go, to perform specific duties determined by your employer, in order to earn a living. You must carry out the duties of your occupation because it is your place of employment.

When "work" is looked at as a verb, you are getting paid for your services, for which you exert a physical or mental effort in order to do, make, or accomplish something. It also means to be effective or achieve the desired result, and to produce results or to exert an influence.

To sum things up, if you approach "work" as a noun, you are just going through the motions because you have to make money to survive. If you approach "work" as a verb, you are investing yourself mentally, physically, and creatively in order to be effective and productive. You take ownership and responsibility and have a sense of pride in the work you do. This is what an artist does when creating a work of art or design or when composing music.

I look at choosing a career in a different way than most people. I believe that you should figure out what it is you love to do, (i.e. something that you would do 24 hours a day, seven days a week if you could) then find a way to make a living doing it. This concept is completely contrary to what society would have you to believe.

The next part of this book asks you to think outside of the box. It may feel uncomfortable at first and some might find it a bit challenging, but if you look at it with an open mind, you will have the ability to create a life that is more fulfilling than you could have ever imagined.

WARNING! Some people will think that you are losing your mind and will try to talk you out of going after your dreams. Don't take it personally; after all, we live in a society that expects you to conform to more traditional ways of thinking. Therefore, you must be ready for the negative comments and negative views about artists.

In an effort to help you realize what you are up against, I have compiled a list of things that I have heard people say about the creative and artistic individual. I call it "The Negative Views of Artists and Musicians."

NEGATIVE VIEWS OF ARTISTS AND MUSICIANS

- Being a musician is not a real job.

- It's hard to make a living - *(The "starving artist")*.

- Musicians can't get a real job - *(That's why they play music)*.

- Musicians are always late.

- Musicians are lazy - *(They don't really want to work)*.

- All musicians drink and do drugs.

- Musicians are just plain weird.

- Musicians party a lot.

- Musicians are unhealthy - *(They don't work out)*.

- Musicians are not business minded - *(They need someone to manage them)*.

- Musicians are egotistical - *(Bigheaded and looking down on other people)*.

- Musicians are unreliable - *(They don't take care of business)*.

- Musicians are a financial risk - *(They don't earn enough money to pay their bills & they have bad credit)*.

- Musicians are not smart.

- Musicians are not responsible parents.

- Musicians are out of touch with reality.

I know that this list can be a little discouraging, but fear not! I have also compiled a list of positive attributes and characteristics of the creative individual, in an effort to eliminate this type of thinking and to give you ammunition to fight off negative people. I called this list "The Positive Views of Artist and Musicians."

John E. Lawrence

POSITIVE VIEWS OF ARTISTS AND MUSICIANS

- Being a musician is a real job if you treat it like a business.

- Musicians enjoy what they do for a living— *"If you enjoy what you do for a living, you will never work a day in your life."*

- Musicians are their own boss and they set their own hours—*you decide when to practice, teach, and hold recording sessions, and decide what performances to accept.*

- Musicians cannot afford to be lazy because they have a multifaceted career.

- Musicians are busy working at the parties; therefore, they are unable to join in with the activities.

- Musicians make as much money as the amount of work they do—*if you need more money, you simply take on more students, more gigs, sell more CDs, etc.*

- Musicians are good business people—*you are responsible for our own income; you are the business.*

- Musicians can get a paycheck every day of the week—*you don't have to wait until Friday; therefore, the phrases "Living for the weekend" or "Thank God it's Friday" do not apply.*

- Musicians don't have to deal with rush-hour traffic—*you can set our own hours.*

- Musicians can dress up to go to work—*you don't have to get dirty.*

- Musicians bring joy to a lot people—*you see their joy every time you perform.*

- Artists are the voice of society; you interpret life and express it through your work—*you are the voice of change.*

- Musicians are some of the most intelligent people in the world.

- Artists do not have a lot of stress in their life—*your art is a stress reliever.*

- Most musicians are responsible spouses and parents—*one of my saxophonists is married with two children and paid for his wife to attend nursing school.*

- Musicians can make more money and in less time than the average corporate worker—*it may take two weeks of working in corporate America to earn what you can make in one weekend as a musician.*

- Most musicians are health conscious—*they stay away from drugs, alcohol, and cigarettes.*

- Most musicians exercise regularly.

- Musicians can acquire a nice house, automobile, musical equipment and anything else they desire.

- Musicians can have more than one career—*some musicians are also lawyers, doctors, and business owners.*

Note: The positive list outweighs the negative list. In other words, there are more reasons you can be successful at what you do, than there are for you to fail. As a matter of fact, it would be a good idea for you to make a list of the reasons why you deserve to be successful and look at it every day. This will override the negative comments you will encounter from people that don't believe you can succeed as an artist.

FOLLOW YOUR DREAM

Literally, define your dream and measure your progress towards it. If you are not getting there, then ask yourself why not? (You cannot blame someone else). The late Mr. Renaldo Obie Benson, one of the original members of the Four Tops, once said: "Get busy doing what you do best because, the talent is there; you just have to bring it out".

REASONS WHY PEOPLE ARE NOT SUCCESSFUL

Lack of vision

Some people are comfortable with where they are in life. This is not a bad thing if they are making ends meet and they are content. It is important to set time aside for creative thinking and visualization. Sometimes we are so consumed in our day-to-day life and focused on earning a living that we don't take time to re-assess our lives to see if we are on the right path. Many people lack vision for the future and in most cases they have gone as far as they will go in life.

Lack of planning

Some people have the vision, but they fail to plan. They start a business venture that fails due to lack of planning. They never do a cost analysis or a business plan that spells out exactly what it will take in order to be successful. When unforeseen obstacles arise, they are not prepared mentally, physically, or financially to handle things. As a result, the business venture fails. Remember, failing to plan typically means you plan to fail.

Lack of discipline

Some people do not want to put the time necessary to make their dreams become a reality. From a musician's point of view, it takes years and several hours of daily practice to become proficient at their craft.

Singer and songwriter Smokey Robinson has written thousands of songs and is arguably one of the best poet/songwriters of our time.

Michael Jackson was an exceptional vocalist and entertainer at a very young age. He was recording million-selling records at the age of nine and through hard work and discipline mastered his craft. He went on to record the top-selling album in the history of the music industry. His album "Thriller" has sold over 29 million copies to date. Michael Jackson was considered to be the best entertainers in the world. *The Guinness Book of World Records* has identified Jackson as the "most successful entertainer of all time". This earned him the title "The King of Pop."

Tiger Woods was ranked the number one golfer in the world for several years and arguably was the best in his field. He is a naturally gifted athlete, but he is also disciplined and practiced every day. Tiger Woods's father once said that Tiger hits one thousand golf balls, seven days a week, without fail and he has been doing this for years.

Michael Jordan used to average 50 points per game. That meant, if the combined team score was 80 points, Jordan would out score the entire team. Jordan would go to the gym every day and practice free throws for hours. By demonstrating this type of discipline, he proved himself to be one of the greatest basketball players ever.

The point that I am making is that some people have a talent and natural ability; they can keep up with the average person without trying hard. Some are content with being average whether it is in academics, business, arts, or sports. There is one fact that remains true, if you want to excel at what you are doing, then you will have to be disciplined enough to work hard. Additionally, if you want to be great and stand out over others, then you will have to work harder and smarter than everyone else.

I once performed at a banquet and the keynote speaker was Dennis Kimbro, the best-selling author of the book "Think and Grow Rich: a Black Choice." This is what he had to say about being average: "Dream big and think big". "Do not be content with being average because, being average means that you are the worst of the best and the best of the worst". When he put it that way, it made me realize that I did not want anything to be average about me.

PLAYING IT SAFE AND TAKING RISKS

Leverage – to build off other big things going on

Momentum – When you are hot: go for it. When you are not, plan and prepare.

Risk is manageable. It's not a bad thing; it's just something to deal with. Get comfortable with it! To learn about risk, get out there and try things. You may make many mistakes, but it's okay, as long as you learn from them.

Someone once said, "The bigger the risk, the bigger the payoff." It would be nice if you could plan every step in life and know that every chance you take will pay off and bring a positive return.

CHAPTER 2

CHOOSING AN OCCUPATION

I have learned that with your talent and skill, there are multiple areas of employment that you can venture into without having to learn something new or seek additional education and training.

For example, if you play the guitar, then it is a natural progression for you to join a band and perform to generate income. But as a guitarist, you should also consider other opportunities to earn money. Think about what happens if there are little or no performances coming in. The following are some ways to keep your finances flowing:

- If you play guitar, then you can record a CD and sell it with the potential of becoming a recording artist.

- If you are proficient at playing the guitar then you can give private guitar lessons and become a guitar teacher.

- If you give private guitar lessons, then you can also teach group lessons which means that you can teach a class on how to play the guitar.

- If you teach a class on how to play the guitar, you can have someone videotape you while teaching, and put together an instructional DVD and sell it.

- If you write down the information that you teach your students in a lesson plan, then you can compile that information and put together an instructional book for publishing.

- If you become a published author of instructional material then that material could be sold worldwide.

- If you have guitar instructional material being sold worldwide, then you can contact guitar and string manufacturing companies in pursuit of endorsement deals.

ASSESSING YOUR TALENTS AND SKILLS

Are you creative, a virtuoso, a performer, or a combination of all of these? What does that say about career direction? Do you understand what it will take to develop your talent?

Sometimes you have to increase your knowledge of a particular area in order to increase your earnings. For example, you can purchase your own recording equipment and learn how to record and produce your own CDs. This eliminates the cost of having to pay for studio time and for a producer. Once you have become comfortable with operating your recording equipment, you can add to your cash flow by renting out your recording studio. You can also offer your services as a studio musician for additional income.

Something else that will allow personal growth is to study songwriting and music composition. You can begin writing and recording music designed for TV and radio commercials (i.e. jingles). There is a lot of money that can be earned for writing jingles.

MAKE A LIST OF THINGS THAT YOU ENJOY DOING

This is how we begin. First make a list of all the things that you enjoy doing. Don't be concerned at this time whether you can make money from doing those things. I want you to feel free to list everything from flying a kite, shopping, going to the movies, playing an instrument, singing, reading, taking pictures, and drawing.

Whatever you enjoy doing should be included on your list. The more items you have on your list, the more opportunity you have to create multiple sources of income, which increases your earning potential.

For example, I will compile a list of some of the things I enjoy doing:

- Playing Pool
- Bodybuilding

- Drawing
- Playing Guitar
- Martial Arts
- Performing
- Teaching
- Landscaping
- Throwing Frisbees
- Cleaning cars

The next step is to write down potential occupations related to each item on the list. For example:

1. Playing Pool: Become a professional pool player.

2. Bodybuilding: Become a professional bodybuilder.

3. Drawing: Become a professional artist.

4. Playing Guitar: Become a professional musician.

5. Martial Arts: Teach martial arts.

6. Performing: Become a professional entertainer

7. Teaching: Teach at an educational institution

8. Landscaping: Own a landscaping company

9. Throwing Frisbees: Compete in Frisbee contests

10. Cleaning cars: Own an automobile detailing shop

The final step is to select an item from your list and figure out how many other jobs are related to that item. This will allow you to see what your maximum earning potential could be. Figure out which occupations would be easiest for you to start working. In order to do this, take an honest assessment of your talent, knowledge, equipment and assets. Make a list of the jobs that you are ready to move into right away, and then list the jobs that you will be able to do later with time and preparation.

The following are examples of jobs that you can do now:

1. Perform with a band

2. Give private lessons

3. Become a studio musician

In order to make each item on this list a reality, you should find other musicians with similar musical interests and goals to perform with a band. Secondly, find your strengths as a musician and teach what you do best to students. Lastly, be able to read music fluently and to play in time, in order to become a studio musician.

The following are examples of jobs that you can do in the future:

1. Studio owner (rent out studio time)

2. Recording artist (sell CDs)

3. Record jingles for TV/Radio

In order to make each item on this list a reality, you should obtain a music production and engineering certificate. Second, develop yourself as an artist, strengthen your producing and arranging skills, and also your songwriting and overall musical skills. This applies to both steps 2 and 3.

THINGS TO CONSIDER BEFORE YOU START GIVING PRIVATE LESSONS

- Put together a good lesson plan.

- You must have patience and good people skills.

- You must be a motivator as well as a teacher.

- You must have a good physical space to teach lessons; a place that offers privacy and safety for the student and yourself.

- Most places that sell musical instruments also offer private instruction. This a good place to start teaching, because they can get students for you. They may take a percentage of the money you bring in, but you will make it up in volume.

- It is a good idea to adopt a policy that states: "All students must pay for their lessons one month in advance and the money is non-refundable." This will prevent students from canceling their lessons just because they would rather do something else that day. It also guarantees income for you.

Note: *If you have never taken private lessons before, I would recommend taking lessons from more than one teacher, in order to pick up on tips of how to be an effective teacher.*

Qualifications for being a studio musician

- Must be able to read music fluently

- Must be able to play with the steady tempo

- Must be familiar with many different styles of music

- Must acquire the necessary equipment (e.g. instruments and effects pedals) to accommodate the producer's needs

Operating your own recording studio

The following is a list of qualifications and things to consider before opening up a recording studio and selling studio time:

- Know how to operate your equipment (your clients are paying by the hour and they do not want to waste time and money by watching you try to figure out how to operate your equipment).

- Record a demo CD that could be used as a representation of the type of sounds your studio is capable of producing.

- Advertise by word-of-mouth (if you do an excellent job for your clients they will spread the word)

- Offer your musical, producing and arranging skills to your clients, at an extra cost, to maximize your earning potential

- Offer a comfortable and nurturing environment to your clients. People choose a recording studio based on how comfortable they feel in their working environment, as well as the sound quality that can be produced.

- Be careful of the clientele that you allow in your recording studio. (Some people will rent studio time to observe your equipment with the intent of stealing it.)

- Be careful how you advertise your recording studio, particularly if it is located in your home. (Again, criminals are always thinking of ways to take what you have worked so hard to acquire.)

- Some very elaborate recording studios with equipment worth millions of dollars, look like abandoned buildings, with no sign that there is a recording studio inside. Owners do this to keep criminals away.

The flowchart

A flowchart will enable you to see employment opportunities based on your talents and skills. A flowchart will also help you to see your earning potential. This is how the flowchart works:

First write down your primary skill or talent. Then write down all of the jobs that stem from that primary skill. All of the primary jobs will have other jobs that stem from those. These jobs are called secondary skills. All secondary skills will generate secondary jobs.

Note: Some individuals will have more than one primary skill or talent. If this is the case, remember to create a different flowchart for each primary skill.

Putting together a flowchart

Here is an example flowchart based on my skills as a guitarist. As you review it, keep in mind that each item in the flowchart represents an additional source of income.

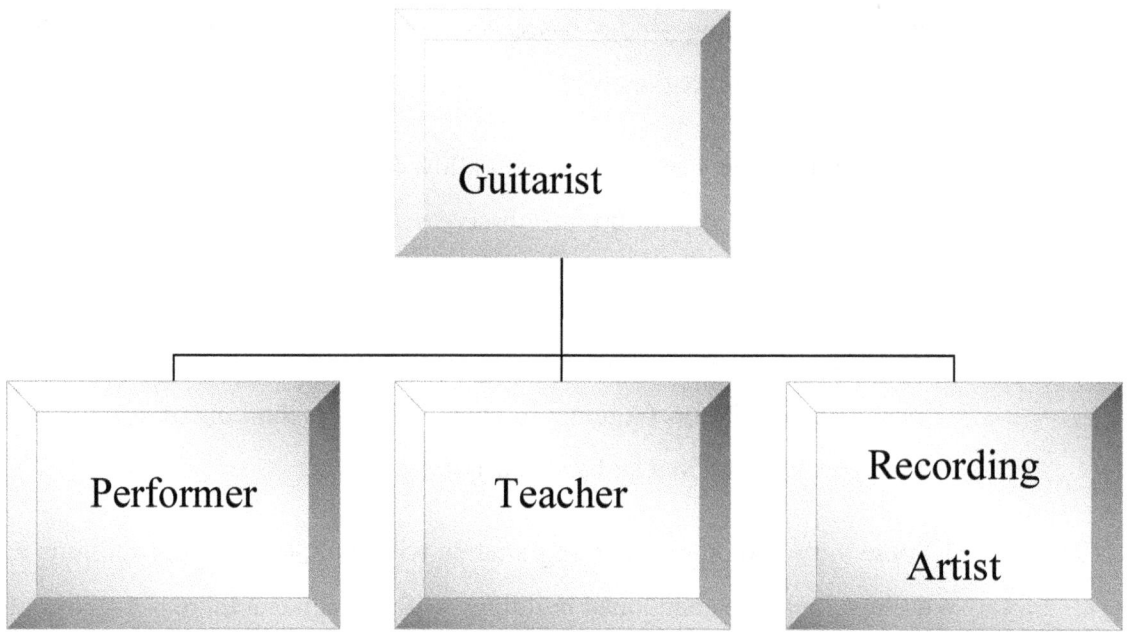

Business Management for the Working Musician

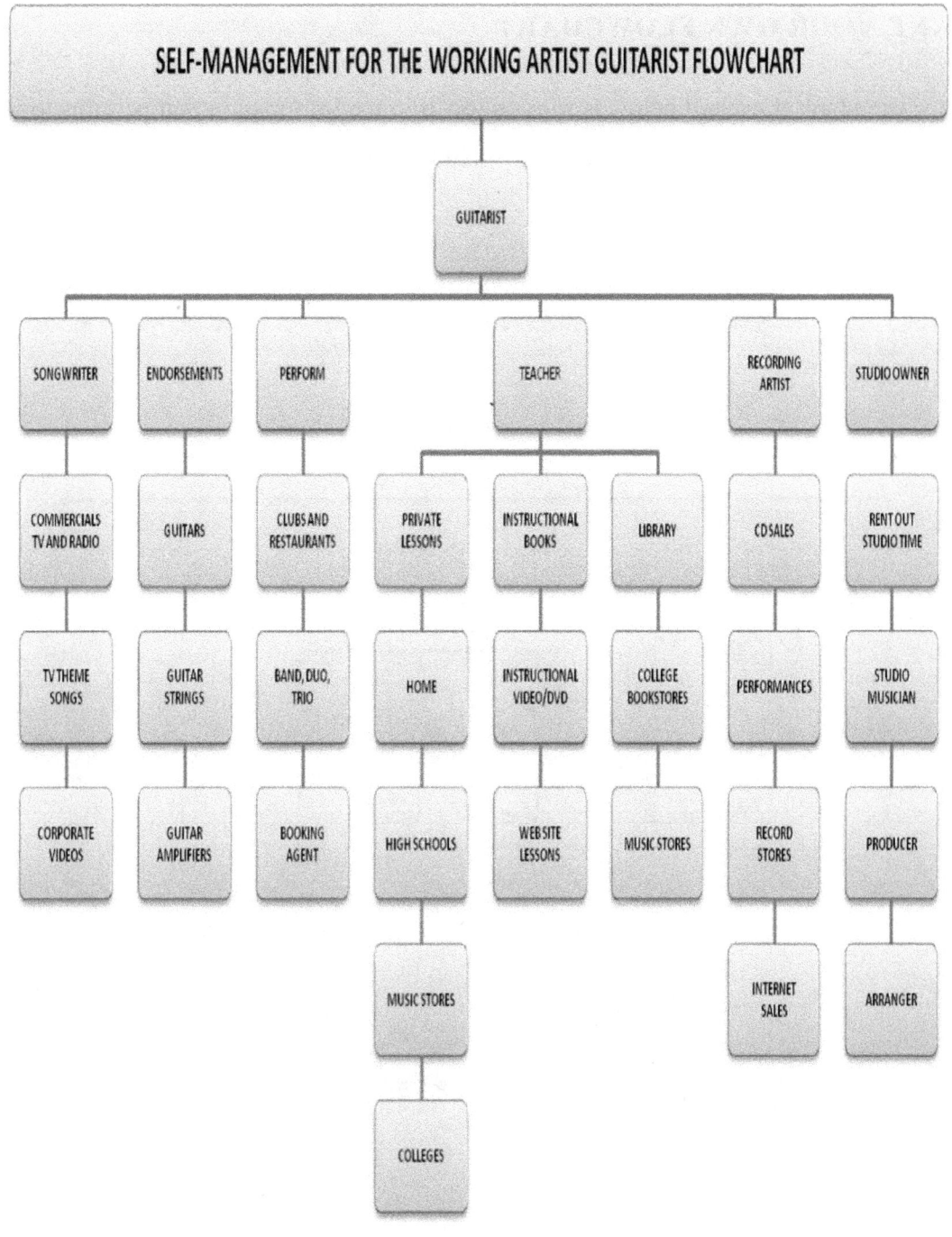

MAKE YOUR OWN FLOWCHART

The blank flowchart below is for you to fill in the information that pertains to your primary skill and talent. Also, remember to include the related jobs that coincide with them.

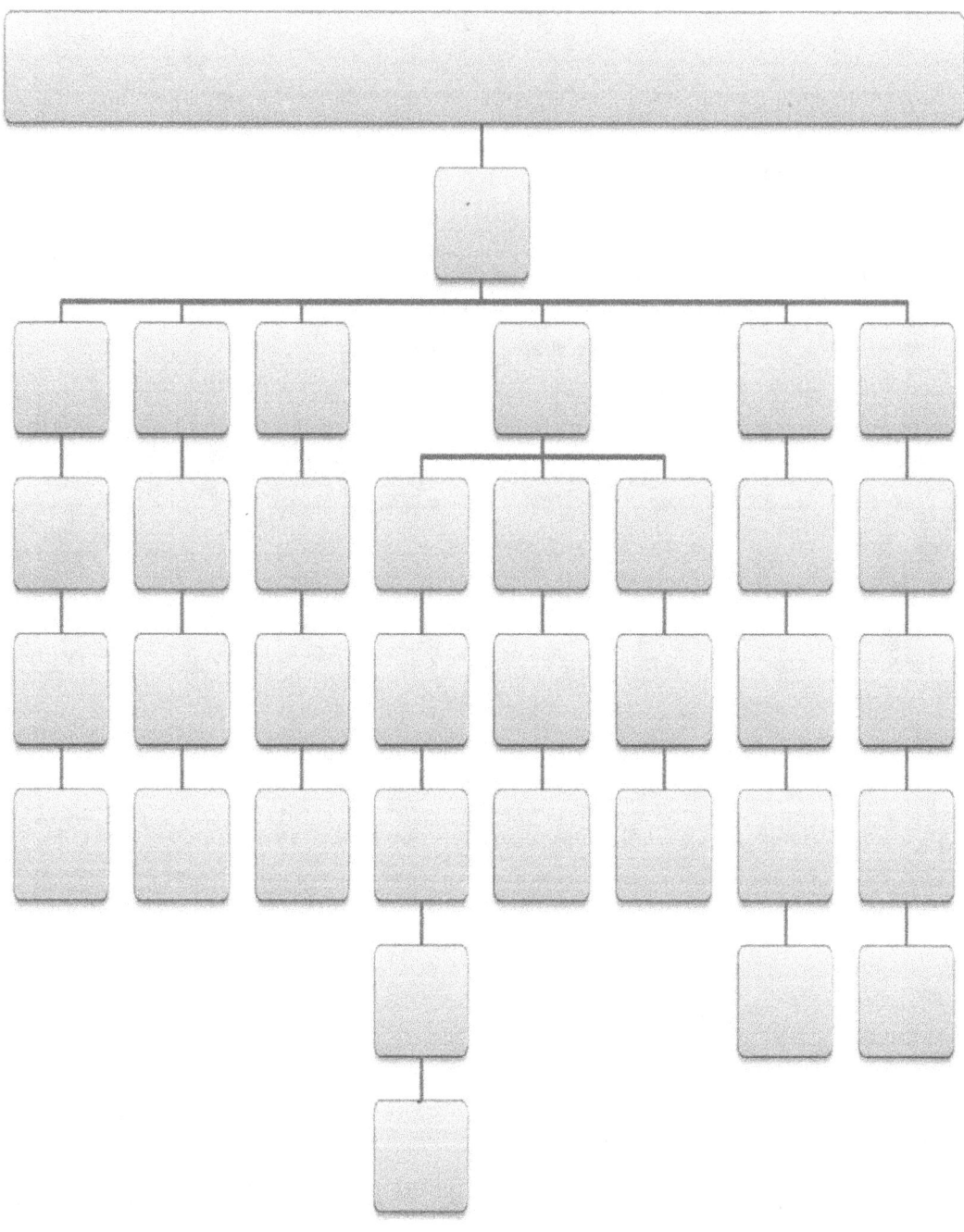

CHAPTER 3

PUTTING YOUR BAND TOGETHER

Some of the qualities you should look for in musicians and singers when putting a band together are:

- Commitment
- Team Player
- Good Attitude
- Flexibility
- Reliable
- Musicianship
- Work ethic
- Reliable transportation
- Good equipment
- Make sure that they don't have any problems such as: drinking, drugs, egotistical, or someone in their life who may not want them in a band or playing music (e.g. a parent or mate).

After selecting the right band members, and while you are considering performing as a professional group, you should also remember that you are starting a business activity involving the exchange of money for services. Your service is excellent entertainment!

John E. Lawrence

EVERY BAND NEEDS A LEADER

I used to be in a band and we all felt that we were adults who could make intelligent decisions. Therefore, we decided there was no need to designate a bandleader. Needless to say, the band did not go very far because we did not make the same decisions. We could not agree on the songs that we were going to play, what gigs to pursue or even what to wear. There is an old saying that goes "too many Chiefs and no Indians". That's how our band could be categorized. Understand there is no shame in being a follower. As a matter of fact, a good leader knows how to be a follower.

There are a lot of "behind the scene" activities that do not require the involvement of the entire band. This is where the bandleader steps in. These activities include:

- Being the spokesperson for the band
- Making calls to booking agencies
- Sending out promo packs
- Scheduling band rehearsals
- Running the rehearsal
- Returning calls to potential clients
- Controlling the overall sound and volume of the band
- Finding and distributing music to band members that will be performed

Note: All of the band members should have a voice in matters like repertoire, wardrobe, equipment purchases, etc., but when a group decision cannot be made, the bandleader should make the final decision.

A bandleader should recognize the strengths, talents and skills of each band member.

A good leader knows how to delegate responsibility and let someone with more experience handle some things. Every leader can use a partner with complementary skills, someone that will tell you when you are wrong and someone that will listen to your ideas.

The following are some examples:

- There may be a band member who has experience working and producing music in a recording studio. That band member should be in charge of producing the demo or any other recordings for the band.

- There may be a member of the band who has an outgoing personality and the gift of gab. That individual should do most of the talking during performances.

- There may be a band member who has expertise in computer graphics. That person should be in charge of designing flyers, posters, and any other material required for the band's promo pack.

- There may be a band member who is familiar with computer programming and Internet web design. Utilize that set skills to create the band's webpage and adding the band on You Tube or Facebook.

Putting together your song list

When putting together a song list, it is important to keep in mind the type of engagements that your band will be performing for. If your band will be performing at clubs, then find out things such as who frequents the club (what age group they cater to) and what style of music is preferred in that establishment. This allows you to put together your song list based on your audience. Learn as many songs as possible. Include the title of songs that you plan on learning in the future. The more songs your band knows, the more impressive and experienced your band looks. If someone requests a song that you don't know, use this as an incentive to learn the song and add it to your show.

Never remove songs from your song list even if you have not performed them in a long time. Allow your song list to grow. You can put your song list together in musical categories such as fast, slow, rock, blues, pop, jazz, and R&B. It may also be helpful to list the song title and artist. When booking performances, the client will get a concept of the type of music your band is able to play.

HOW TO MAXIMIZE YOUR REHEARSAL TIME

If your band is made up of musicians who have never played in a band before, then it is a good idea to practice what everyone enjoys playing. Some of the things that you should be learning are:

- Playing in tune

- Keeping a steady tempo

- Controlling the volume of the band

- The overall blend of the band

- Developing a good stage presence

- Equalizing your instruments

- Discovering the proper sound to use for each song

- Communication skills

- Learning to communicate musically

When I was in my early teens, I was in a band called the "Soulful Soulmates." We used to rehearse from 6:00 PM to 9:00 PM Monday through Friday. We learned all of our songs by ear. There were two reasons for this. In the mid-60s, it was hard to find sheet music for some of the popular R&B songs and anyway, no one in the band could read music. Everyone would gather around the record player and learn their parts.

It was a slow and sometimes a very frustrating process, but we got the job done. We would learn about two songs per rehearsal. Looking back, it was not the best way to utilize rehearsal time. Now that I am older and wiser, I maximize rehearsal time by giving each band member a list of songs to work on in advance. I supply them with a CD and whenever possible, the sheet music. It is each band member's responsibility to show up at the next rehearsal ready to perform the songs.

The advantage to learning songs this way is that you increase productivity. Instead of averaging two songs per rehearsal, now the average is 10 songs. Instead of learning the songs at the rehearsal, you can concentrate on song arrangements, putting the show together, and choreography.

When you give song assignments in advance, it's easy to tell who is serious about the band and who is not. If someone shows up consistently without learning the songs, you may consider replacing them because learning the songs is not a priority to them. They are not only wasting your time, but also the other band members' time. As a matter of fact, I use the method of giving out assignments to my band members as a means of weeding out those individuals who are not serious about performing with me.

Here is a simple way I select vocalists and musicians before I even rehearse with them. I ask them to send me a list of songs they already know. I do this to put together a show that consists of songs that we both have in common. Surprisingly, most will not make it past this part of the selection process. Individuals who don't send me their song list eliminate themselves from being chosen.

The best thing about using this method is that you don't have to fire them or give an explanation why they are not right for the position. Most individuals will not call back and inquire about working with me because they haven't done their part.

PERFORMING WITH A MUSIC SEQUENCER

Performing with a music sequencer makes it possible for an artist to perform to soundtracks without the use of live musicians. Artists can perform to background music tracks that they programmed themselves or purchased online.

The tracks are programmed on a MIDI workstation or computer using music software such as "Reason" or "Cakewalk." Programmed music is another way of saying music that is recorded electronically. One person can program all of the musical instruments in a particular song, which usually consists of bass and rhythm guitar, keyboards, drums, strings, and a horn section. Once all of the parts are added and mixed down, you can perform using these tracks and even record with the same sequences.

Of course, performing with soundtracks has some advantages and disadvantages. Some advantages are:

- You have the option to perform as a solo, duo or trio act and charge just as much as a five or seven-piece band. This is a strong advantage because there are fewer personnel to pay therefore; you can easily increase your income. Let's take a closer look at what that means. If you are making $25,000 yearly, at $100 per performance, then for the same number of performances, you potentially could increase your income from $25,000 to $125,000 a year.

- You don't have to deal with individual's schedules, attitudes and poor work ethics.

- You can fit into a full performance space, which increases your options for places to perform.

- You can develop a more polished act because there are no mistakes in the

Business Management for the Working Musician

music track. This allows you to focus in on perfecting your playing.

- You can present a more professional sound because you have total control over the volume. You have the ability to produce the sound of an orchestra or full rhythm section.

- You can cut back on rehearsals. Give the other musicians copies of the soundtracks so they can practice their parts on their own time. Schedule one or two rehearsals prior to the performance.

Note: I don't recommend giving out high-quality recordings of the soundtracks because other musicians may use your soundtracks at other performances without your knowledge.

Some of the disadvantages of performing with soundtracks are (Note: *I have included my comments to each disadvantage listed)*:

- Some individuals believe that performing with the music sequencer puts musicians out of work.

- (*Comment*) There are enough jobs and money to go around.

- It takes time to put music tracks together.

- (*Comment*) It also takes time to put a band together.

- If you decide to purchase music files it can cost a lot of money.

- (*Comment*) You will recoup the money that you invest in the music tracks within your first two performances. Consider purchasing music tracks as an investment.

- You have to follow the same song structure each time you perform the songs.

- *(Comment)* Most good bands do that because they want the song to be recognizable.

- You must have a good PA system to play the soundtracks through in order for them to sound realistic and professional.

- *(Comment)* Every band should have a good PA system.

- The people that you work with should have a good sense of timing, especially the drummer, in order to perform to the soundtracks.

- *(Comment)* If you cannot keep good time then you should not be on stage performing anyway.

- You must really know the soundtracks in order to prevent you from getting lost.

- *(Comment)* A true professional knows where they are and what is going on within the song at all times.

CHAPTER 4

ASSESSING YOUR BAND'S WORTH

Do people want the music you created, or do they simply value your ability to perform background music or dance music? Assess your worth from the point of view of your customer, not of yourself. It doesn't matter if you believe that your music is worth $XXX/performance if the club or concert promoter calculates that your value to his business is less.

I have a very simplistic way of deciding how much to charge for a performance. I simply ask myself this question, how much money would it take for me to feel that I have been properly compensated at the end of the night?

Let us take a look at what is involved in doing a performance.

- Learn the material individually.

- Practice the material with the band.

- Put a show together.

- Book the performance.

- Notify the band of the performance.

- Preparation on the day of the performance.

- Load equipment.

- Drive to the performance.

- Unload equipment.

- Set up the equipment at the venue.

- Do a sound check.

- Perform three to four sets of material.

- Load equipment back into your vehicles.

- Drive home after the performance.

- Unload the equipment.

How much money would you need to be paid for a performance? What amount of money would make you feel like it was worth everything that you had to go through in order for you to do the job? Whatever that amount is, that is what you should be charging.

Here is something else to keep in mind when determining the price for your work. Add up the amount of time you have put in becoming proficient at your craft. Your years of experience should be factored into that amount. For example, a person that has been the playing guitar for three years should not charge the same as someone who's been playing for twenty-five years. Don't be afraid to use your years of experience when negotiating your price. A number to start with, is to pay everyone in the band at least $100 per performance. As the band becomes more established, the price will go up.

In the 1970s, jazz clubs and restaurants that had entertainment, paid musicians $60 - $75 per person to perform for 4 hours. In many cases, the prices have not changed. Although there have been pay increases literally in every occupation, due to inflation and the increase in minimum wage, some musicians are still playing for the same pay 40 years ago. Why is this?

The cost of everything has gone up, food, gas, musical instruments, automobiles, rent, houses, utilities, clothing and furniture. The price has increased as much as 10 times that of what it used to be in the 1970s. Musicians who are still being paid 1970s wages for their services, are having a hard time making ends meet. It's no wonder that there are starving artists in the world today. Therefore, in order for an artist to make a living in today's world, they must charge today's prices.

Putting together your price list

One thing that has helped me to get the pay I feel I deserve for a performance has been to put together a price list. In it, I itemize all of the different ways that I can perform and then put a price on each one. I then provide a brief description of what I offer for each item. Below is an example:

Price List

Plan A: Solo Guitar

This plan is recommended for soft background music for receptions, dinners, and wedding ceremonies. This plan is also appropriate for settings where audiences want to just sit and listen to quality music.

My price is *$200.00* per hour.

Plan B: Solo Guitar with a Sequencer

The sequencer provides the sound of a full band accompaniment. This is good for the client who wants a full sound of a band but does not have the budget to pay for a full band. This plan is recommended as a soft musical background for receptions, dinners, and wedding ceremonies.

My pricing starts at *$350.00* for the first hour, and *$200.00* for each additional hour.

Plan C: Guitar and Sax Duo with Sequencer

The saxophone adds variety to the sound as well as adding to the musical selections.

The price starts at *$500.00* for the first hour and *$250.00* per additional hour.

Plan D: Guitar, Sax, and Vocalist or Keyboard with Sequencer

By adding a vocalist (male or female), the performance becomes more of a show. This plan is recommended for banquets and dances.

My pricing begins at *$850.00* for the first hour, and *$300.00* per additional hour.

Plan E: Four-piece Band with Sequencer

This plan consists of integrating guitar, saxophone, keyboards, and drums. Note: A male or female vocalist can be substituted for the keyboards and drums. Having two vocalists increases the variety of musical styles the band has to offer. Recommended for dances, concerts, and wedding receptions.

My pricing begins at *$1,000.00* for the first hour, and *$350.00* per additional hour.

Plan F: Five-piece Band

This band consists of Guitar, Saxophone, Keyboards, Bass Guitar, and Vocalist, (male or female). By adding the additional members, the show is enhanced by the visual as well as musical effect. I recommend this plan for dances, concerts, and wedding receptions.

My pricing begins at *$1,150.00* for the first hour, and *$400.00* per additional hour.

Plan G: Nine-piece Band

You will experience the ultimate in live entertainment when your performance includes guitar, keyboards, drums, bass guitar, and a three-piece horn section (saxophone, trumpet, and trombone), with a male and female Vocalist. This plan is designed to provide fullness of sound and an exciting visual effect. With this plan, we can keep the audience dancing all evening.

Pricing begins at *$2,550.00* for the first hour and *$550.00* per additional hour.

Please Note: I require a 50% non-refundable deposit on all bookings. Any bookings farther than 45 miles away may be subject to additional travel and lodging fees.

There are many advantages to having a price list. One thing that I have noticed is that people who contact me for a performance honor my price list. I believe this is because the costs of my services are clearly defined in writing. Another reason why people don't try to talk me down is because of the different options I offer. If one plan is not affordable, then they can choose a plan that best fits their budget. Regardless of which plan is chosen, I am always in the in the plan.

Price Negotiation

Listed below are things to remember when someone wants to hire your band.

- Never agree to a price without having your price list.

- If someone approaches you at a performance and inquires about the cost of your band, always avoid quoting them a price. Instead, ask them for an e-mail address or fax number so that you can send them your price list.

- Always speak with confidence when quoting your price, act as if the price that you are quoting them is no big deal, even if the price that you are quoting is more money than you have ever charged before.

Don't feel bad if someone turns you down because they feel your price is too high. It just means they did not have the budget for your band at that time. It does not mean that there is something wrong with you, your band or the way you have negotiated. You can't take it personally!

I can remember the first time someone turned me down for a job because they felt my cost was too high. I felt bad and started thinking that "some money is better than no money" and maybe I should have lowered my cost. After thinking about it, I realized that some people will not be able to afford my services. Just as a person who wants to buy a new car and their budget is about $15,000-$20,000 goes into a Cadillac dealership to buy a car that costs $50,000, they have to realize a Cadillac is not within their budget at this time. It doesn't mean that the salesperson did something wrong or there is a problem with the automobile.

You know what your band is worth. You should not be charging the same as a band with less experience or one that does not bring the level of professionalism to their performance.

Here is a sample contract:

Business Management for the Working Musician

AMERICAN FEDERATION OF MUSICIANS OF THE UNITED STATES AND CANADA
(Herein called "FEDERATION")

CONTRACT
(Form C-1)

Whenever the Term "The Local Union" Is Used In This Contract, It Shall Mean The Local Union Of The Federation With Jurisdiction Over The Territory In Which The Engagement Covered By This Contract Is To Be Performed.

THIS CONTRACT for the personal services of musicians on the agreement described below is made this 4 day of June 2010 between the undersigned purchaser of music (herein called "Purchaser") and the undersigned musician or musicians.

1. Name and Address of Place of Engagement:

2. Name of Band or Group:

3. Number of Musicians:

4. Contact person:

5. Dates(s), Starting and Finishing Time of Engagement:

6. Type of Engagement (specify whether dance, stage show, banquet, etc.):

7. Compensation Agreed Upon (Amount and Terms):

8. Purchaser Will Make Payment As Follows:

9. Special Instructions:

IN WITNESS WHEREOF, the parties hereto have hereunto set their names and seals on the day and year first above written.

_____   _____
Print Purchaser's Full and Correct Name   Signatory Musician

X _____   X _____
Signature of Purchaser (or Agent thereof)   Signature of Signatory Musician

_____   _____
Street Address   Street Address

_____   _____
City   State   Zip Code   City   State   Zip Code

_____   _____
Telephone   Telephone

_____   _____
Booking Agent   Agreement No.   Address

Name of All Musicians	Local Union No.	U.S. Social Security No.	Direct Pay
MUSICIAN-1	_____	_____	$_____
MUSICIAN-2	_____	_____	$_____
MUSICIAN-3	_____	_____	$_____
MUSICIAN-4	_____	_____	$_____
MUSICIAN-5	_____	_____	$_____
MUSICIAN-6	_____	_____	$_____
_____	_____	_____	$_____
_____	_____	_____	$_____

CHAPTER 5

HOW TO GET A GIG

How do you get gigs? This is a question that I'm often asked by students. There are many ways in which an artist can find employment and I will share some with you. Let's assume that your band is well rehearsed, and you have enough material for a show. The next step is to put together a promotional pack or promo pack. This is a packet that is a professional representation of your band. An important part of the promo pack is the bio, which is a biographical description of your band. The following explains the purpose of a bio and offers some helpful tips on preparing one.

PREPARING A BIO

A bio is a document that basically outlines your past, present, and future achievements. It lets the reader know who you are and your life story as it pertains to your music career. It usually is condensed into a one-page document. Some of its uses are:

- It introduces you to potential employers.

- It informs the news media of who you are.

- It is a method to assess your productivity.

It is not necessary to include every aspect of your life into your bio; however, you should write about the highlights of your career.

Here is a tip: When putting together your bio, stay away from sounding negative. For example; a student wrote in his bio that he was in a rock band for five years, but they broke up because the lead singer started to ego trip and was too difficult to get along with.

I told him that it was not important to focus on the way the band broke up. Instead he should acknowledge that he was in the band for five years and emphasize what he gained from that experience. I also told him that he could have said that he was in a Rock Band for five years. During that time they were able to build a repertoire of fifty of the most popular rock songs of that era. Also, he was able to improve his rhythm and lead guitar skills, while gaining knowledge of how to put together a stage show and appreciate the importance of developing a good stage presence. Instead of sounding negative and bitter, I was able to bring out the positive aspects of that experience. Some students feel that they have not accomplished enough in their lives to put together an impressive bio.

Here is some advice I offer my students. Write down what you do, whether it's playing an instrument, singing, producing, or arranging. Explain what interest you have about it and how long you have been doing it. Write about some of your major influences, about what styles of music you prefer and why. Also include things like the type of study or work you are doing to improve your talent or skills (e.g. taking classes or private lessons; acquiring a certificate or degree; working as an intern in a recording studio to gain practical experience).

The following are examples of two famous artists' bios.

John E. Lawrence

THE FOUR TOPS

The Four Tops

The Four Tops have been marveling audiences with their infectious blend of pure vocal power and sweet harmonies since 1954. High school friends from Detroit's North End, Levi Stubbs, Renaldo "Obie Benson, Abdul "Duke" Fakir, and Lawrence Payton started working in local night clubs as The Four Aims. During a brief stint with Chess Records in 1956, they changed their name to The Four Tops so as not to be confused with the popular Ames Brothers. In 1960 they signed with Columbia Records for another brief record release session. After catching the eye and ear of Billy Eckstine and traveling with Billy working major nightclubs and venues, they returned to Detroit in 1963 to sign with their friend and the owner of Motown Records, Berry Gordy.

At Motown the group was teamed with the songwriting powerhouse of Holland, Dozier, and Holland. The rest, as they say, is history. Hit after hit followed, starting in 1964 with *"Baby I Need Your Loving"* and continuing with songs like *"Reach Out, I'll be There," "Standing In the Shadows of Love," "Bernadette,"* and *"I Can't Help Myself*

(Sugar Pie, Honey Bunch)." During the British music invasion of the USA, The Four Tops becomes a sensation in England.

In 1972, after Motown moved to Los Angeles, The Four Tops signed with ABC/Dunhill Records. The group hits kept on with *"Ain't No Woman (Like the One I've Got),"* *"Keeper of the Castle,"* and others. As records sales started slowing, the group returned to their strength, the live show. While the hits may not have been coming as fast, they played to audiences all over the world, maintaining the vocal magic that had placed them in the upper echelon of the entertainment world.

In the early 1980's, The Four Tops signed with Neil Bogari and Casablanca Records. Two albums on the label produced the hits, *"When She Was My Girl"*, *"Tonight I'm Gonna Love You All Over"*, and *"I Believe In You and Me"*. In 1985 the group stopped the show at the heavily rock filled LIVE AID concert. Critics around the world hailed their set as a highlight of the marathon benefit concert. But benefits were not foreign to The Four Tops. To this day, they have raised money all over the globe with their charity work, never forgetting where they came from.

The hits stopped coming during the late 1980's, but the group continued playing almost 200 dates a year and ended the decade by being inducted to the Rock n' Roll Hall of Fame in 1989.

Solo work has never been something that The Four Tops set their sights on, but on occasion they have lent their talents to others. Lawrence and Duke served as producers on other music projects, Obie co-wrote *"What's Going On?"* with Marvin Gaye and Levi was the voice of the man-eating plant, Audrey II in the movie, *"Little Shop of Horrors."*

But through it all, the group stayed together for 43 years, something that is unmatched by any other group ever. Nothing could stop them, not even the bad times and hardships of the entertainment world.

In June of 1997, Lawrence Payton died of liver cancer. The group decided to continue on and worked for almost 2 years with just the 3 remaining members, with no signs of slowing down, dedicating every show to the memory of Lawrence Payton.

1999 marked the group's 45th anniversary, and also the first member change. In February, Theo Peoples, a golden voiced, multi-talented young man from St. Louis, and Ronnie McNeir joined Obie and Duke onstage for the first time. The result has been magic, and shows that the group is ready to continue playing concerts, corporate events, and even performing 80 symphonies to spread their special magic worldwide.

ASHFORD AND SIMPSON

Ashford and Simpson

The renowned duo of Nickolas Ashford and Valerie Simpson has been described as one of the most prolific, versatile, and exciting musical couples in recording history. Their career as performers, songwriters, and producers spanned more than three decades. The popular husband and wife team collected 22 gold and platinum records and more than 50 ASCAP Awards, including the prestigious Founders Award for outstanding contribution to and influence on popular music. Since their collaboration began in 1964, Ashford and

Simpson created an unprecedented catalog of chart topping hit singles and albums, including tunes like "Solid," "Is It Still Good To Ya," and "I'm Every Woman." Many performers have recorded their songs, including Diana Ross, Chaka Khan, Whitney Houston, and Gladys Knight and the Pips.

The couple met in 1964 at White Rock Baptist Church in New York City. It was there that Valerie played and sang with the Church's legendary choir. After Nick joined the choir, the two began writing pop songs for fun and a career was born, it was at Scepter Records that Ashford and Simpson wrote their first hit single, "Let Go Get Stoned." The 1964 classic tune, recorded by Ray Charles, brought the R&B duo to the attention of Motown. After joining Motown as staff writers, the hit-making team wrote their second smash hit single "Ain't No Mountain High Enough" for Marvin Gaye and Tammi Terrell. That was soon followed by other unforgettable Gaye/Terrell hits, such as "Your Precious Love," "Ain't Nothing Like The Real Thing," and "You're All I Need To Get By."

In 1973, Ashford and Simpson signed with Warner Brothers as recording artists. They recorded nine albums for the label – three of which were gold – and numerous hit singles. After their contract with Warner Brothers expired, the couple recorded five more albums with Capital Records in the 1980's. In 1996, the singing/songwriting team partnered with Poet Maya Angelou to produce the album "Been Found." Ashford and Simpson's own production company, Hopsack and Silk Productions, on their own Hopsack and Silk Record Label, released the album.

This dynamic couple, who were married for over 20 years, enjoyed one of the most long-lived musical partnerships in recording history until Nick Ashford's death. Even more remarkable is the fact that they built their career focusing on primarily one topic: love. "I get bored when I'm not writing about love," Ashford admits. "Love lifts me up," he says, "so that's why I deal with it". It is no wonder that their career and lives together remained "solid as a rock."

Putting together a promo pack

Put together some type of representation of what your band looks and sounds like, so when you're talking to potential clients, they do not have to take your word for how great your band is. This can be accomplished by putting together a promotional package, also called a promo pack. The promo pack should consist of nine essential items:

- Demo CD or DVD
- Professional photo
- Bio
- Song list
- Business cards
- Newspaper or magazine articles about you or your band
- Reviews about your CD
- Reviews of performance
- Endorsements literature

Song List:

- 2 BE AS 1
- A SONG FOR INGA
- A SONG FOR MY FATHER
- AFFIRMATION
- AFTER THE LOVE HAS GONE
- AIN'T NO MOUNTAIN HIGH ENOUGH
- AIN'T NO WOMAN LIKE THE ONE I GOT

Business Management for the Working Musician

- AIN'T NOTHING' LIKE THE REAL THING
- ALL BY MYSELF*
- AMAZING GRACE
- AMERICA
- AS
- BATTLE HYMN OF THE REPUBLIC
- BETCHA BY GOLLY WOW
- BIRD OF PARADISE*
- BIRDLAND
- BLACK ORPHEUS
- CALL ME
- CHIPMUNK CHRISTMAS
- CHRISTMAS TIME IS HERE
- DANCING IN THE MOONLIGHT
- DIDN'T I BLOW YOUR MIND
- DON'T YOU WORRY 'BOUT A THING
- ELLIE'S LOVE THEME
- EVERGREEN
- EVERLASTING LOVE
- FEEL LIKE MAKING LOVE
- FOR OLD TIMES SAKE
- FOR ONCE IN MY LIFE
- FOR YOUR LOVE
- GIRL FROM IPANIMA
- GIVE LOVE ON CHRISTMAS DAY
- GOD REST YE MERRY GENTLEMEN
- GOING UP YONDER
- HARK THE HAROLD ANGELS SING

John E. Lawrence

- HE KEEPS DOING GREAT THINGS
- HOME*
- I SAY A LITTLE PRAYER
- I WANT YOU BACK
- I WISH
- IF YOU DON'T KNOW ME BY NOW
- I'LL BE THERE
- I'LL REMEMBER CHRISTMAS
- I'M SO PROUD
- ISN'T SHE LOVELY
- JAZZ-O-NOVA*
- JESUS IS THE ANSWER
- JINGLE BELLS
- JUST TO SEE HER
- KILLING ME SOFTLY
- KNOCKS ME OFF MY FEET
- L SAMBA*
- LET'S DO IT AGAIN
- LIVING INSIDE YOUR LOVE
- LOVE WON'T LET ME WAIT
- M.A.S.H.
- MISTY
- MOON RIVER
- MORNING AFTER
- MOTHER'S LOVE*
- MR. BO JANGLES
- MY CHERI AMORE
- MY FAVORITE THINGS

Business Management for the Working Musician

- NEVER CAN SAY GOODBYE
- NEVER GO BACK*
- OH HAPPY DAY
- OH CHRISTMAS TREE
- OVERJOYED
- PEACEFUL LIVING
- REACH OUT AND TOUCH
- REACH OUT I'LL BE THERE (FOUR TOPS)
- RIBBON IN THE SKY
- ROCKET LOVE
- SAY YES
- SILENT NIGHT
- SINCE I LOST MY BABY
- SO THIS IS PARADISE*
- SOMEWHERE OVER THE RAINBOW
- SPINNING AROUND
- STANDING IN THE SHADOWS
- STOP LOOK LISTEN
- SUNNY
- SUPER WOMAN
- THAT'S THE WAY OF THE WORLD
- THAT'S WHAT FRIENDS ARE FOR
- THE LOOK OF LOVE
- THROUGH THE FIRE
- TOMORROW (THE WINANS)
- TOUCH ME IN THE MORNING
- TRACKS OF MY TEARS
- UNTIL YOU COME BACK TO ME

John E. Lawrence

- WAY BACK HOME
- WE'VE ONLY JUST BEGUN
- WHAT A WONDERFUL WORLD
- WHAT'S GOING ON?
- WHITE CHRISTMAS
- WINTER WONDERLAND
- YOU AND I
- YOU MAKE ME FEEL BRAND NEW
- YOU WILL KNOW
- YOUR SON

JOHN E. LAWRENCE BIO

John E. Lawrence, a lifelong resident of Ypsilanti, is one of Michigan's most talented and respected guitarists. John is now gaining national recognition with his recent contract with *Mel Bay Publications, Inc.,* one of the country's largest publishers of instructional materials. Mel Bay has produced for John a videotape entitled *"Jazz Improvisation, Walking Bass Lines, and Chord Melodies."* Released in the summer of 2001 are three companion instructional books with compact discs (CD's) which include *"Improvising Solos for Guitar," "Walking Bass Solos,"* and *"Chord Melody Solos."* The books and CDs can be used alone or in conjunction with the videotape. John's most recent accomplishments include contracts to endorse *Heritage Guitars, Takamine Guitars* and *La Bella Guitar Strings.* He is also featured in *Mel Bay's "Collector's Edition Anthology of Jazz Guitar Solos."* This collection features solos by some of the world's finest jazz guitarists. John has also written two articles in Mel Bay's Internet magazine, one titled *"Practice is the key to musical success,"* and the other titled *"Blues Improvisation"* for March and April 2000 issues.

Mr. Lawrence credits his musical talents first and foremost to God, then to the late Dr. Morris J. Lawrence, Jr. (no relation). Dr. Lawrence was an instructor and chair of the Music Department at Washtenaw Community College (WCC). Under the tutelage of Dr. Lawrence, John was challenged and inspired to continuously improve his skills as a guitarist. Following in the footsteps of his mentor, John became an instructor at WCC where he has taught for 27 years and is presently the Director of the Music Performance Program. In less than two years, he has developed over twenty-five new courses and three new Certificate Programs. In 2008, Washtenaw Community College awarded John with the Morris J. Lawrence award; which is the highest honor given to a faculty member. John also developed the "Living Legends Series." The series provides a stage for famous recording artists to be interviewed and share their life stories in front of an audience. This is followed by a question-and-answer period and a concert. Washtenaw Community

John E. Lawrence

College students have an opportunity to receive firsthand knowledge from musical legends. The series has hosted artists such as: Mavis Staples, The Four Tops, Ashford and Simpson, Earl Klugh, and the Temptations. John has been the opening act for the series and performs with most of the artists as guitarist and director of the Living Legends house band. In 2007, the Dean of Humanities and Social Science, Dr. Bill Abernethy, awarded John with the "Living Legend Award" for successfully completing five years of the series.

In the realm of performance, Mr. Lawrence served as musical director and lead guitarist for vocalist Carl Carlton, who opened for such famed artists as Smokey Robinson, Chaka Khan, Lionel Richie and the Commodores, Rick James, Teena Marie, and Frankie Beverly and Maze.

Among Mr. Lawrence's many accomplishments is a performance at Carnegie Hall. In addition to touring throughout the United States and performing at Jazz Festivals such as: Boston Globe, New Orleans, and Montreux Detroit, he has also performed in Haiti, Surinam, Germany, and the Montreux Jazz Festival in Switzerland.

John has made television appearances on three nationally syndicated programs: *Kelly & Company*, *PM Magazine*, and *Good Morning America*.

One of Mr. Lawrence's most memorable occasions was with legendary jazz guitarist, Mr. Kenny Burrell. Mr. Burrell asked John to sit in with him at the famed Baker's Keyboard Lounge in Detroit, Michigan. After the performance, Kenny commended John on his playing ability.

John's sound recordings include "The Supreme Dream," "Old Smooth," "Summer Nights," "All By Myself," "Merry Christmas from John E. Lawrence," "Winter Wonder Land," and "A Solo Guitar Christmas."

For more information, please e-mail him at johnelaw@wccnet.edu.

Business Management for the Working Musician

Demo CD

There are some things to keep in mind when putting together a Demo CD. Think variety when you are deciding on songs to include on your demo. Include up-tempo medium and slow songs. The songs should demonstrate your versatility while displaying your strengths. The demo does not have to be more than three to four songs in total.

Other things to keep in mind when putting together a demo to get gigs:

- Put your best song first. Keep in mind that people are very busy, so they may not listen to the entire CD. Therefore, you have to grab their attention within the first fifteen seconds of listening.

- Restructure the songs so that the best part of each song is heard first.

- Stay away from long introductions. You may get rejected before the verse starts.

- Do not include original material. Save your original material for when you are putting together a demo to get a record deal. Remember people will judge your band based on how well you perform songs with which they are familiar.

- Some bands put together a medley of songs which means they record shortened versions of the songs. This enables them to record 7 to 10 short songs in the time it takes to record four complete songs. This is how it works. Record the introduction, first verse and chorus only. You can transition into the next song or fade each song out after the course. Bands can show more variety this way.

- Put together your demo so that it looks professional. Remember the more professional you package yourself, the more money you could ask for.

- Include an insert in your CD case complete with song titles and track information.

- Always include booking information on the insert and on the CD itself. *(Band leader's name and phone number, e-mail address and website etc.)*

- Make sure that your CD is well recorded and produced because it may be the only representation of your work that the client will hear.

- Never be afraid to invest money into recording a demo. If you receive three bookings as a result of someone listening to your demo, then you have recouped your investment.

DESIGNING YOUR BUSINESS CARD

When you are designing a business card for yourself or your band, keep it simple and clean. Be sure to use a font that is legible. If you have more than one talent or business, keep them separate. Do not try to save money by incorporating all of your service offerings on one business card. Most will assume that you cannot be good at everything, even though you have more than one talent.

Business Management for the Working Musician

John E. Lawrence Artist Business Card Example

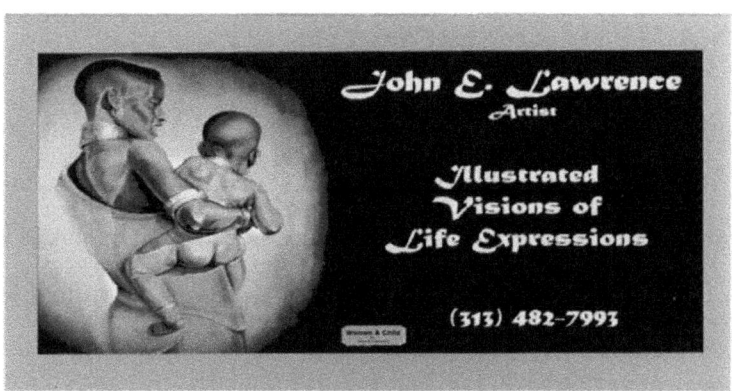

MAKING YOUR CONTACTS

Once you have your promo pack together you can begin contacting venues where you would like to perform. They can include:

- Night clubs and Casinos

- Restaurants

- Concert houses

- Hotels

- Festivals

- Booking agencies

- UAW Locals

- Colleges and universities

- Corporations and other businesses

- Wedding planners

- Churches

PUTTING ON A MUSICAL SHOWCASE

A good way to attract potential clients is to put on a "musical showcase" and invite representatives from the above list to come see you perform. The showcase can be held at a nightclub, an auditorium, restaurant, or other venues. Some bands will hold this type of event for their CD release party. You may consider charging a nominal fee at the door to help offset the cost of sponsoring this event.

Publicize the event well, invite everyone you know and ask them to bring a guest. Be sure to invite local media personnel including TV, radio, newspapers, and magazines. Your potential clients will be impressed with the amount of people that attend your event. Be sure to have plenty of promo packs on hand.

You can also hire professionals to video tape and audio record the event, so you can have a DVD and a live CD made. The DVD and CD can be used to promote your band. Also, you can sell them at future performances to generate additional revenue. It is also a good idea to hire a professional photographer to shoot pictures of the event. Remember the key is to hire professionals because you don't want to end up with material you are unable to use.

HOW TO KEEP A GIG

Now that you know how to get a gig, the next step is how to keep a gig. It is important to find out what type of musical service the client would like you to provide before you accept the engagement. You must ask questions such as:

- What type of function is it? *(Ask this question to find out if your band is right for the function.)*

- Will there be dancing? *(You need to know this so you can structure your show to have primarily up-tempo dance music.)*

- What type of music are they looking for? *(Ask this question so you can adjust your repertoire to fit the occasion.)*

- Would they prefer the band to be the focal point or background music? *(Jobs have been lost because there was not a clear understanding between the band and the client. Also, some functions require both formats.)*

- *If you are performing at a wedding reception, the client might want your band to play soft music during the cocktail and dinner hour and more up-beat party music during the dance portion of the evening.)*

- What is the primary age group and general makeup of the audience you will be performing for? *(This is an important question because you will need to tailor your show to please the audience.)*

- What size room are you performing in and approximately how many people will be attending? *(This is an important question because you will need to know what type of equipment to bring to accommodate the occasion.)*

FINDING THE RIGHT GIG

Note: Sometimes the client asks for a particular type of music for their function but the people attending the function want something different. For example, someone once hired my band to play at a function and they specifically asked for Jazz. He said that there would be one thousand business men and women attending the function that enjoy jazz, so our band would be perfect. When we started to play, the audience wanted to dance! They wanted to dance, electric slide and hustle to the most current R&B music! We tried to accommodate them by changing the tempo and the style of the songs we had in our repertoire.

After the first set, we were approached by the individual who hired us. He informed us that he had found an emergency DJ for the rest of the evening, since the audience wanted to dance. We did receive our full pay and the rest of the band members were happy because they were done performing. As a band leader and businessman, I was disappointed because it appeared that we were unprepared and could not provide the service we were hired to do.

The reason why I ask the above questions is to try to avoid this from occurring again. I found that sometimes as a bandleader, I have to inform the client of the type of music and band that will work best for their function.

Remember to match yourself to the right venue and constantly work on improving your performance. Plan for growth and measure your progress toward the next "bigger" gig.

WORKING WITH A BOOKING AGENCY

Booking agencies can be another resource for finding performances. They work on the premise that they will receive a percentage of each performance they book for you. This is not a bad idea in theory. The booking agent will book your band at an agreed upon price and then add a 15% booking fee to the total cost of the performance, which is passed on to the client. For example, if a booking agent has a performance at $500, the total cost would be $575. You would receive your asking price (i.e. $500) and the booking agent would receive their percentage (i.e. $75).

Sometimes a booking agent may call you with a performance that pays below your normal asking price. My advice is to take the performance. A good booking agency will book you enough times throughout the year, so you will make the money up in volume. At the end of the year, your income would be greater than it would have been if you only accepted higher-paying gigs.

Most booking agents are also musicians and singers. This is a good and bad thing. Since they are musicians themselves, they tend to work hard for you because they understand that this is your livelihood. On the other hand, if there is a higher-paying performance, they will reserve the right to book it for their own band.

Some bands will sign an exclusive contract with a booking agency. This means that they can no longer deal with any other agency and they are not supposed to book themselves. If a client wants to hire their band, they are supposed to refer the Client to the booking agency. If the band books a performance outside of the booking agency, they are required to pay 15% to the booking agency.

I would avoid signing an exclusive artist contract with a booking agency until you are completely satisfied with their work. Some of the things to look for when considering working with a booking agency are:

- Do they have a reputation for treating their artists fairly?

- Can they find your band constant work?

- Do they book the type of performances your band requires?

- Are they easy to work with?

- Are the agents honest and professional?

- Do they pay the type of money that your band requires per performance?

It is not common for the agency to make you wait until they receive payment from the client before they issue you a check. This could take from 3 to 5 business days, but the payday should be consistent each week.

When you are working with an agency, they will give you business cards with your band's name, the agency's name, the booking agent's name, and the agent's contact information. You are expected to pass out these when you are at a performance booked by the agency. Some bands try to bypass the agency by using their own personal business cards. This is not a fair practice because, if the agent had not booked the performance, you may not have met the client in the first place. Another reason to use the agency's business card is, it makes you look more professional when you say that you have an agent working for you. Save your personal business cards for performances that you book without the use of the agency.

Most booking agencies are respectful and honorable organizations, but there are some agents that take advantage of their artists. The following are some things to be careful of:

- Some agents will tell you that the client is paying a certain amount to the agency and will pay you a percentage based on that amount, but in actuality they have charged the client much more. For example; the agent tells you that the performance will pay you $500 and the client is paying the agency $575 but in actuality the client is paying the agency $1500 and the agency is keeping $1000 and paying you $500.

- Some agents will tell you that business is slow, and they don't have any performances for you. They may actually be keeping the performances for their favorite bands.

- Some agencies will hold on to your paycheck for weeks at a time. This buys them time to pay other bills so they can stay in business.

- Some agencies will issue bad checks that cannot be cashed, due to a lack of funds in their account.

- How do you know if a booking agency is reputable? The answer is simple. Ask other musicians about their experience working with the agency.

Musicians will let you know if they have been treated fairly or not. They will let you know which agents to work with and which ones to avoid.

Do you really need a booking agency? I have been booking myself for many years and I have always had performances. However, I have found that there are some commercial establishments that prefer working with an agency. It saves them the hassle of auditioning entertainment and they can offer a discounted rate on the artist.

Here's how it works. The booking agent will contact a club or hotel and work out a deal that they will supply them with quality weekly entertainment if they will allow the agent to book their establishment exclusively. If the agent can land contracts with ten different hotels or nightclubs, then they can do quite well financially. It works out well for everyone that is involved, the band, the agent, the club and the audiences. If you want to play those rooms, then you have to go through the agency.

THINGS YOU SHOULD KNOW ABOUT PLAYING CLUBS

Club engagements do not pay as well as private or corporate parties. The reason is that a client that hires your band for a private or corporate party will pay what you are asking. A club owner might hire your band two to five nights per week and you may repeat engagements throughout the year. This is called a multiple booking discount. The amount of the discount can be negotiated, but on average, you can plan on lowering the price to at least half. If your band wants to get top dollar for their performances, they should concentrate on private or corporate functions. However, there is a disadvantage, because it is very difficult to build up a following. The only people that will see your band perform are those that are invited to those functions.

My advice is to book as many private parties as you can and on the dates that you have open, book the club dates. This will help your band build up a following. If your band is good, then you owe it to your audience to perform at places they can attend.

Most clubs will book bands one week and rotate them between seven to ten bands. If you are in the rotation, this means that on average your band will perform at an establishment once every two to three months. Therefore, if your band wants to perform regularly, then you need to find at least seven to ten clubs to work at and get into their rotation schedule.

Something else to keep in mind is that most clubs cater to specific audiences. This means that they only book entertainment that their clientele will enjoy. This is why you never see a jazz band performing at a club that attracts heavy metal or rock audiences. It is not a matter of how good your band is, a club owner will not book your band if you do not play the type of music that caters to his clientele.

Conduct a search to locate all of the clubs in your area, and then find out the genre of music they cater to. Your band may even have to travel to different cities. Decide on how far your band is willing to travel to do a performance. If your band has to travel more than two hours, you may want to negotiate the cost of lodging when booking your engagement. If a hotel or club owner is not willing to include this expense, then you may have to turn it down.

THE MORE MUSIC YOU KNOW THE MORE OFTEN YOU CAN WORK

You can increase your band's marketability by being more versatile in your repertoire. For example, if your band specializes in R&B, then it would not be difficult to add pop music. This would expand possibilities for employment. There are other musical genres that are similar in style and will utilize some of the same musical techniques and characteristics. There are many similarities between blues and traditional gospel music. All of them incorporate the same type of chord progressions, quarter tones and microtones. They also utilize similar rhythms. It would not be too difficult to perform in different bands that cover these styles of music. Rock and Roll utilizes some of the same skills and musical techniques as Blues, Jazz Contemporary or Smooth Jazz and Latin. They all share similar chord progressions. Remember, the more you expand your repertoire, the more opportunities there are for employment.

HOW TO PUT TOGETHER A SHOW

It is necessary to keep the audience in mind when you are putting together your show. Think about the age group that you will be performing for. If your audience is made up of people from the ages fifteen to twenty then be sure to include songs that they can relate to. This usually means the songs from the current pop, rock, hip-hop, and R&B charts.

If your audience is made up of an age group ranging from twenty-five to forty-five, keep in mind that they have been around longer and listening to music longer. Therefore, you need a wider range of music in your repertoire that includes hit songs ten to twenty years ago. Also, it is a good idea to include songs from the current charts.

If your band is planning on performing at wedding receptions, then they should understand that all of the bride's and groom's relatives and closest friends will be in attendance. This usually means an audience of all ages. Therefore, you must plan on including songs that everyone can relate to.

THE TRUTH ABOUT WHY SOME MUSICIANS CANNOT FIND WORK

Some musicians and singers cannot find work because they are bringing something other than their talent to the table. Some have a bad attitude, and no one wants work with them. Although they may be a good musician or singer, their attitude is enough to drive people away.

Others cannot find work because they have a problem with punctuality. They are late for everything, classes, appointments, rehearsals, and performances. They are not late because of an emergency or something beyond their control. They are just in the habit of not allowing enough time to make it to their destination. I think the best way to get my

John E. Lawrence

point across is to tell you about some real-life situations I have encountered.

True Story 1: I Want My Money

The first story is entitled "I Want My Money"

I once had a weekly gig, performing as a duo, on Wednesdays from 6:00 p.m. until 8:00 p.m. at a local university for their Jazz Series. I hired a female saxophonist that I had worked with in the past. I was very impressed with her sound and stage presence. On the first performance, she arrived an hour late and missed the entire first set. I was concerned that something had happened to her, maybe car trouble or a car accident. I was expecting an apology or an explanation of why she was so late, but she said nothing.

We started the second set, and she didn't play like she had in the past. At the end of the performance, she came to me for her pay. I asked her how much money was she expecting to receive, considering that she only worked half of the night. She said, "All of my money." I could not believe what I was hearing, so I explained to her that the performance was from 6:00 p.m. until 8:00 p.m. and she only played an hour, half of the gig. I asked her, "Don't you think that you should receive half of your money?" She replied; "No, I want all of my money." I chose to pay her for both sets, but I never called her again for a gig.

Let us examine what happened. The gig paid $100 for two hours. She walked away feeling that she had gotten the better end of the deal because she received full pay for working half of the job. Now let's take a look at the big picture. She never offered an apology or explanation of why she was an hour late. She also demanded that she be paid in full for providing half of the services she was hired to do.

If she had offered an apology or explanation of why she was late and displayed a different attitude about her pay, I would have continued to work with her. Just working with one individual, she could have potentially earned thousands of dollars over the next few years, but instead she settled for $100. That was not a good business or financial decision in my opinion. Some people focus more on what they can get now than what they can get in long run. I offer this advice: *"Live in the now but work toward your future."*

The irony is that individuals like her often feel they have done nothing wrong. They continue their same pattern throughout their lives, and one day they realize they can't find any gigs. The truth of the matter is, they run all of the gigs away!

True Story 2: A Tale of Two Musicians

I call this next story "The Tale of Two Musicians"

I have a friend who opened a local upscale restaurant. He was looking for two solo acts to perform. One would perform on Saturday evenings and the other on Sunday evenings. I recommended a guitarist who could perform on Saturdays and a keyboardist that could perform on Sundays.

The guitarist worked the gig every Saturday for three and a half years. The keyboardist was let go after one month. Before I explain what happened, I want to clarify that between the two musicians, the keyboardist was more accomplished.

Now, this is what happened. The keyboardist did three things wrong that lost him the job. First, he did not show up the second week of the engagement. When I asked him why, he explained that no one called him for the following week. I explained that this was an ongoing engagement, every Sunday, unless otherwise notified. He understood and said that he would be there each Sunday going forward.

Here is the second thing that the keyboardist did wrong. There was a mutual agreement between the restaurant owner and musicians that they could order one dinner, at no charge, whenever they performed. Each Sunday, the keyboardist would bring his wife to the restaurant and order two dinners. He never paid for the other dinner he was responsible for and therefore it cost the restaurant money.

John E. Lawrence

After the fourth week, I asked the owner how the keyboardist was working out. The owner told me that he would take breaks for 45 minutes to an hour. The owner said that out of a three-hour engagement, he was only getting about 45 minutes of playing time from the keyboardist. Strike three he was out! He was let go after four weeks.

When I asked the restaurant owner how the guitarist was working out he answered, "Just fine". He said that the guitarist played good music at a volume that allowed the customers to enjoy their meals and conversation.

He also said that the guitarist was a nice guy and always arrived about an hour and a half before time to perform. He would set up his equipment, sit at the bar and order juice or a soft drink, and relax. Five minutes before starting time, he would strap his guitar and be prepared to play on time. His sets lasted 45 minutes and he only took two fifteen-minute breaks throughout the evening. He was polite to the customers and the wait staff. They were all are very pleased with him. The guitarist's name is Michael Moore and I have asked him to put together a short bio and give some advice to my students.

MUSICIAN MICHAEL MOORE: BIO AND ADVICE

I've been a musician most of my life and I guess I've always had a thing about people not keeping their word and not doing what they said they would do. I'm also a bit of an obsessive compulsive so things just have to be so with me and I'm a little bit of a stickler about following the rules whatever they happen to be. I'm on meds now so I'm a little better under control about waiting on other people.

I started out in public safety in 1976 as a cadet with a suburban police department where I stayed for three years transferring to the fire department in 1979. From 1979 to 1999 I was late for work on only two occasions. In 1999, I knew I would be eligible to retire in 2004 so for the last ten years of my career (1996-2006) I never took a sick day.

This was all part of my plan which started when I took over for John E. Lawrence, who was performing at a cigar bar in Grosse Pointe, Michigan. What I thought was going to be a short stint wound up being very successful eight years with the Andiamo Restaurant group (a very successful restaurant chain in Metro Detroit), and countless other major gigs.

After this eight-year run, I chose to go out on my own and again John Lawrence came through. While subbing for him at the Quarter Bistro in Ann Arbor on a Thursday night, I got the Saturday night gig, which lasted for three and a half years.

My longevity in all of these situations I chalk up to my own principles and some common sense. I am NEVER late to anything! No matter what it is, no matter who it is. I feel it is showing a total disrespect to whoever you are keeping waiting, and you are no more important than they are. In the eight years I was chief of the Inkster Fire Department I was never late to a meeting, function, or anything that required my presence. Get to the gig early enough to set up, get your set lists together, warm up, and relax for a minute.

- Do not drink on the job! Most musicians like to drink while gigging, but if something goes wrong alcohol can easily be blamed and you can get a reputation quickly.

- Be humble and act professional! Don't act as if you are doing management a favor by playing at their establishment. Don't beg, but don't be a jerk either, and don't forget to thank them.

- Don't take long breaks! I try to plan my set list before I leave for the gig. I do a full hour for the first set, so I finish at the top of the hour, and then take my breaks accordingly. This way I finish the night at the top of the hour.

- Don't take advantage of Comps! If you are doing a restaurant gig and they give you meal comps, don't order the most expensive thing on the menu "to go!" Order something cheap and quick! They pay attention to the bottom line.

- Keep your mouth shut! If you gossip about anyone at the establishment, it will get back to them!

- Be friendly and mingle! Often patrons will give you complements on your breaks, always smile, and be polite even if you are in a bad mood. If you take a seat at the bar and they strike up a conversation, always talk to them; never brush them off even if you have other people there to see you.

- Say what you mean and mean what you say! Don't say you are going to show up with person "A" then show up with person "B" without notice or promise a four-piece group and show up with a three-piece group. There should be no surprises!

- Be selective about stragglers! Yeah, we call it gigging, but this is a job. If you are working in a plant, you don't bring your girlfriend or boyfriend with you to work. Make sure it is okay before you bring others with you. Some places are so busy you may need reservations.

Business Management for the Working Musician

- Watch your language! This one is obvious! Also try to stay away from politics or religion. You don't know who you may offend or who they may be related to.

Back to my plan, which was to retire from the fire department and draw a full pension; then gig, run my studio, and record label full time which would make me more money than I was making while working full time at the Fire Department. But then recession hit...oops!

THINGS EVERY MUSICIAN SHOULD KNOW

I have been playing the guitar for over 46 years and during that time I have learned and experienced things that l would like to share with you in hopes that they will help you as you build your career.

- The best musician does not always get the job.

- It is not how complicated a song is that makes it a good song, it is how good it sounds.

- Play what is right for the song, not what is right for you.

- Every part of a song is important no matter how simple it might be.

- Find your own voice and develop your own style.

- You do not have to have the best musicians in your band in order for your band to be the best.

- Practice with your band to improve the band's sound and practice alone to improve your individual sound and overall musicianship.

- Every band member can be replaced so don't think that you have to put up with attitude problems for the sake of keeping the band together.

- Watch out for the club owner or the person who says, "If you work for me at a reduced price for the time being, I will increase your pay when business picks up." This usually never happens.

- Know the primary function of your instrument as it pertains to the band.

- Do not invite your friends and family to your performances unless they are open to the public, such as festivals, concerts, and clubs, and expect them to pay admission.

- Do not limit your search to find employment as a musician to clubs and concerts. I have performed in some interesting places over the past forty-five years. Take a look at the list below and ask yourself this question, would I have thought to look for performance opportunities in these areas?

- Department stores

- Banks

- Basketball games

- Hotels

- Corporate functions

- Marathons and Walk-A-Thons

- Art galleries and museums

- Luncheons

- Retirement and Birthday Parties

- Retirement homes
- On a yacht
- School functions
- Churches
- Graduation ceremonies
- Chamber of Congress functions
- Bridal and baby showers
- Weddings
- Furniture stores
- Bowling alleys
- Grocery Stores

CHAPTER 6

CONTACTING RECORD COMPANIES

There are many ways to introduce yourself to people or companies that you are interested in doing work with, but I recommend putting together a letter of introduction. I prefer this method because it is a professional way to let people know that you are a viable person in the work force. It is an inexpensive way of promoting yourself. It is a also a way of obtaining permission to send a promo pack. Once you have written your bio, you can take excerpts from it and put together a letter of introduction.

PUTTING TOGETHER A LETTER OF INTRODUCTION

A letter of introduction should include:

- The person's name and company that you are sending it to.
- Information about yourself and what you have to offer.
- Your reason for contacting them.
- What you hope to gain from working with their company.
- What you have to offer their company.
- Thank them for their time and consideration.
- Your contact information.

SAMPLE LETTER OF INTRODUCTION

Hello, my name is John E. Lawrence,

I am a professional guitarist. I have achieved many levels of success in the music business. I have instructional books published by Mel Bay Publications, along with an instructional Video. I was included in the Jazz Anthology 2000 book which features Guitar Solos by some of world's finest Guitarists. I am the director of the music performance program at Washtenaw Community College in Ann Arbor, Michigan. I have guitar endorsement deals with Takamine Acoustic Guitars and Heritage Electric guitars. I have had guitar string endorsements with GHS strings and am currently endorsing LaBella strings. One of my books is "Chord Melody Solos," which received a favorable review in the 2002/2003 Jazz Times Magazine.

I am writing this letter to inform you that I am in pursuit of a major record contract. I have recorded five CD's to date in the contemporary jazz style. I own the masters and have published them under my own label. I have sold thousands of units and am now looking for a distribution deal with a company that will take my products worldwide. If this is something your company would be interested in, please take a moment to view my website at johnelawrence.org and listen to some of my material. I can be contacted at 711-555-7777 or e-mail me at johnelaw@wccnet.edu.

Thank you for your time and consideration.

Sincerely,

John E. Lawrence

CREATING A DEMO CD

A demo CD demonstrates the musical ability of the band or individual. It can be used to get performances or to generate interest from record companies. A good demo should be tailored to accompany its purpose.

For example, when putting together a demo CD for the purpose of getting a performance, the music should be all popular songs. The demo should also show that you can perform a variety of styles. The goal is to try and sound as much like the original recording as possible. Your client will be comparing your demo to the actual recording for a point of reference. This is why it is not a good idea to submit original material on your demo CD.

If you are putting together a demo CD for the purpose of landing a recording contract, it should be prepared differently. The demo should be comprised primarily of all original material. The reason is that record companies are in the business of making money by selling music. If a song has been previously released on another record label, then someone else owns the publishing rights. The record label that you are dealing with will have to pay money to obtain a license to record and release the songs. In essence it will cost the company more money than they are willing to invest into your project. This is why record companies primarily deal with artists that have original material.

The industry standard for the number of songs that should be on a demo CD is three to four. The goal is to record something that will capture the listener's attention as soon as they hear it.

The following are some tips for preparing a demo CD for the purpose of obtaining a recording contract:

- Place the best song first to get the listener's attention right away. If the first song doesn't grab their attention immediately they may not listen to the rest of your CD.

- Avoid long introductions. Save that for the finished product.

- Structure the songs in a way that the best part of the song is heard first. People in the music industry can tell whether or not they like the song within the first few seconds of listening. This should not be a surprise to you. Think about when you're scanning the radio stations in your car, when you are trying to find a song that you like. How much time do you give each station before changing it? Put your demo CD together with that in mind.

- Show versatility but stay within the particular genre of music. Record executives like to categorize artists. When they're listening to your demo they are thinking about things like: does your music fit the image, is it marketable, and most important, will people buy your CD? All of these things translate into whether they can make money with you.

There are two schools of thought when it comes to attracting the attention of a record label, old school and new school:

Old School: there was a time when a recording artist had to have their own style or voice. If someone sent in a demo and they sounded like Beyoncé for example, the A&R Director would say, "There is already a Beyoncé out here and we do not need another one. Try again when you have your own style."

New School: if someone approached a record label these days with the same scenario, the A&R director would say, "She sounds just like Beyoncé and Beyoncé sells a lot of records. There is a chance that the new artist will do the same and she would be offered a recording contract."

The old school way of thinking is prevalent in the movie "Ray" the Ray Charles Story. When Ray Charles was recording in the studio, the record executive stopped the recording session and told Ray Charles that he sounded just like Nat King Cole, and they did not need another one.

CHAPTER 7

JOHN E. LAWRENCE'S STEPS TO SUCCESS

Learn to do as much as you can as it pertains to your business. *The more skills you develop the more jobs you will be qualified for which will increase your earning potential.*

Have a sense of urgency. *Most people approach their goals and life as if they had all the time in the world. Set goals and go after them as if your life depended on it, because it does!*

Be able to perform by yourself, you can fit into more people's budget and more people's physical space. *You can always add musicians. Whether you perform as a duo, a trio, or a quartet, there is always one common thread: you are always in the equation.*

Be able to adapt to change. *If you want to keep on getting what you are getting, keep on doing what you are doing.*

Believe in yourself. *Even when no one else does, it is that belief that will keep you going through hard times.*

Stay way from negative people. *One negative comment can affect you more than 50 positive ones.*

Be conscience of your health. *You need to be healthy in order to do the type of work you're going to do.*

Come early to be on time. *Expect the unexpected—accidents happen, traffic jams happen, and people sometimes change the program.*

Look the part and wear the right clothes for the engagement. *Dress for success.*

Think positive—don't talk yourself out of trying things—go for it. *Expect the best because you deserve it. Expect the best because it is psychosomatic. When you talk to yourself, think positive thoughts because you are listening.*

Don't let money be your motivating factor for why you do what you do! *Let the love for what you do be the motivating factor for what you do. I would not want a doctor to perform an operation on me who became a doctor just for the money. I would rather have a doctor who loves helping people and loves his work.*

Find something you could do 24 hours a day if it were possible. *If you enjoy what you do for a living than it is <u>not</u> WORK! Someone once said, "If you love your work, then you will never work a day in your life."*

Keep your goal in front of you instead of behind you. *Then you won't live in the past bragging about what you used to do.*

Celebrate your achievements and successes, and then move on to the next project. *This will make you a more productive person.*

Set time aside for creative thinking and planning and for setting goals for the future. *Every great idea started as just an idea! If you don't have time to think creatively you will miss out on your opportunities.*

You can tell when you're getting ahead when you come under fire. *There are a lot of people in this world that don't want to see you succeed and they will try to do things to discourage you.*

Work hard and work often. I*t takes hard work to be outstanding in your field.*

If you want to keep getting what you're getting, keep on doing what you're doing. *If you want to achieve something you've never achieved before, then you must do something you've never done before. You must strive to keep growing and learning as long as you live. The moment you think that you know it all, that's the moment you stop growing.*

John E. Lawrence

Get started! Start from where you are. *You don't have to be great to get started, but you have to get started to be great.*

Stick with it until you work it out. *Most people give up on the dream to soon. You never know how close you are to a breakthrough.*

It is the journey as much as it is the destination. *There is no one thing that you will do in life to make your dreams a reality. It will be a culmination of things.*

FINISH WHAT YOU START

A good habit to have and the first step to developing a winner's attitude is to finish what you start. A lot of people have good ideas but very few people act on them. Make a list of all the ideas that you ever had. From that list, make a list of the things you have finished. If the two lists don't balance out, then make it a point to finish the items on your first list. Most people don't pursue their dreams because they let others talk them out of it, and unfortunately, a lot of times we will talk ourselves out of trying our ideas. How many times have you had an idea and you talked yourself out of trying it? You say things like: "it probably won't work anyway" or "it's not a good idea". The ultimate negative thought is: "who am I to think that I could do something like this anyway". We have to watch how we talk to ourselves, because we are listening! It does not matter if people say, "it can't be done because it has never been done before" or "others have tried and failed".

I believe that some things are meant for you to do and no one else. I believe that if it has not been done before, it's only because you have not done it yet! You have to go out and achieve greatness! Write down your goals and start making your dreams a reality.

Dr. Bill Abernethy, Dean of Humanities and Social Science at Washtenaw Community College, once said: "Johnny, you have a lot of good ideas and that's not uncommon. A lot of people have good ideas, but what makes you different is that you make them happen."

An example of following through with an idea is a production that I started called the "Washtenaw Community College Living Legend Series". On the following pages is a copy of the Living Legends Series brochure, which explains my concept in more detail.

THE LIVING LEGENDS SERIES

The Living Legend Series combines the best of Inside the Actor's Studio with Austin City Limits, presenting in-depth interviews with artists on their lives and artistry, followed by a performance in front of an intimate and animated audience.

All proceeds from ticket sales go back to support the Living Legends Concert Series and the Music Performance program.

John E. Lawrence

THE LIVING LEGEND SERIES
Firsthand education from those who have shaped our musical culture

78

Business Management for the Working Musician

The Living Legends Award is offered to those rare recording artists whose music has become part of the soundtrack of our culture. Recipients' names are enshrined in the Washtenaw Community College (WCC) Wall of Musical Fame, and videotapes of their visiting assistant instructors in teaching the principles of music.

Founded by jazz great Dr. Morris Lawrence, WCC's world-renowned music program that has graduated such musicians as:

- Steve Bray: co-composer of four songs on Madonna's "Like a Virgin" album

- Jessie McGuire: lead trumpet for Tower of Power, who was featured playing the national anthem during the 2002 World Series

- David Mann: saxophonist for Tower of Power

- Mark Hines: saxophonist for the New York Symphony

- David Manley: guitarist for Jill Scott

ABOUT WASHTENAW COMMUNITY COLLEGE (WCC)

WCC enrolls more than 12,000 students annually, many of whom are pursuing a career in the music industry. WCC offers more than 30 courses in music performance including: voice, piano, guitar, audio recording, music sequencing, sound reinforcement, theory and self-management. Our faculty teaches students the skills necessary to make a living doing what they love and not to become "starving artists".

- The Venue

Towsley Auditorium is a state-of-the-art venue with approximately 500 seats.

John E. Lawrence

Equipped with the latest in sound and acoustical equipment, Towsley is the perfect place for artists to connect with their audience.

WHO'S BEHIND THE PROGRAM?

The Living Legend series was created as a means of recognizing the lifetime contributions of some very special recording artists. It also provides WCC students and friends a rare opportunity to have close encounters with their idols. "The Living Legends Series is the culmination of the work that goes on during the semester in the Music Performance Program," explains John E. Lawrence, the program's director. "Our goal is to continually create a music program that is both educational and practical, to equip students with the necessary tools and knowledge to survive in today's music industry. I believe this series will take music education to new heights."

John E. Lawrence, leader of the Living Legends house band, is one of Michigan's most talented and respected guitarists. As director of WCC's Music Performance program, he is carrying on the innovative traditions of the late Dr. Morris J. Lawrence, Jr., the beloved chair of WCC's Music Department until his death in 1994.

While a student under Dr. Lawrence (who's no relation to John Lawrence), John was challenged and inspired to continuously improve his musicianship, lessons he continues to pass along to a new generation of students.

A working musician, Mr. Lawrence has performed at Carnegie Hall, the Montreux Jazz Festivals in Switzerland and Detroit, and many other venues around the world.

He's appeared on the nationally televised shows Kelly & Company, PM Magazine, and Good Morning America. He's worked with Atlantic Records recording artists Straight Ahead and served as musical director for vocalist Carl Carlton. He's shared his considerable knowledge with others via instructional videos and books offered by Mel Bay Publications, including Improvising Solos for Guitar, Walking Bass Solos, and Chord

Melody Solos. He appears alongside many legendary jazz guitarists on the Master Anthology of Jazz Guitar Solos, Volume One.

John E. Lawrence's CDs include:

- The Supreme Dream
- Old Smooth
- Merry Christmas from John E. Lawrence,
- Summer Nights
- Winter Wonder Land
- All By Myself, A Solo Guitar Christmas.

His accomplishments have laid the foundation for an explosive career in today's music industry.

For more information:

Contact John E. Lawrence

Phone: 734-677-5146

Email: johnelaw@wccnet.edu

or visit our website at: www.wccnet.edu/livinglegends

DEVELOPING A WINNER'S ATTITUDE

Do what you say you are going to do and be the kind of person that people can count on. You will build a reputation that will make people want to work with and help you accomplish your goals. This is the type of businessperson that people will hire time and time again.

There are certain traits that winners possess. Some people have these traits naturally and it comes easily to them, while others have to make a conscious effort to develop them.

The following is a list of some of the traits that winners possess:

- Winners expect to win because they feel they deserve to. They put in the necessary time to develop their skills. They work harder than most, therefore they exude confidence.

- Winners finish what they start.

- Winners never make excuses.

CHANGING YOUR HABITS

It has been said that if a person can do something for 90 days straight, it becomes a habit and they can do it for the rest of their life. A person needs to change habits that are counterproductive or prohibiting them from attaining their goals. The following is a list of some common habits that prevent people from achieving their goals:

- Procrastination is a bad habit that some people have. They have goals and dreams that they continue to put on hold. They either run out of time to complete the task or they simply lose interest and are no longer motivated to pursue their goals.

- Some people develop the habit of always being late. Being late for appointments can cause others not to work with you because it shows a lack of respect for their time.

- Some people never finish what they start. They have good ideas, but they never see them come to past.

EXCUSES ARE FOR LOSERS

Do not make excuses for your shortcomings. All you are doing is giving yourself an excuse to fail. Think about it when you watch a boxing match on TV. When the loser is being interviewed after the fight, they always have an excuse for why they lost. They say things like: "I didn't try hard enough" or "I didn't stick to my fight plan" and sometimes they will say things like "I just couldn't get started."

When the winner is being interviewed after the fight, they say things like: "I felt great, I trained hard and I stuck to my fight plan and it all came together". They never have to make excuses because they were victorious.

DO NOT HAVE A VICTIM'S MENTALITY

Some people are always blaming others for where they are in life. If something does not work out for them as planned, they never ask themselves what part they played in the failure. They never look at what they could have done differently that would result in a different outcome. Therefore, they are subject to make the same mistakes over and over again. If everyone says that you are wrong, then it warrants taking a look at yourself. Take a look at yourself and if is necessary, make a change. The change may need to occur in the way you operate or maybe your attitude.

TAKE RESPONSIBILITY FOR WHERE YOU ARE IN LIFE

Someone once said: "We are the sum of all of the decisions that we have made in our lives." Where we are or are not in life is the direct result of our decisions. If this is true, then we have no one to blame but ourselves for are shortcomings.

EXAMINING THE SEVEN LEADERSHIP QUALITIES

Coercive power- Involves threats and / or punishment to influence compliance. Example: Using your position as band leader and threaten to kick band members out if they don't show up on time.

Connection power- Based on the user's relationship with influential people. Example: I would use your name and come to you to get things done for my career because you know people like the president of the college, or in music because of the connection you have with music producers.

Reward power- Based on the user's ability to influence others with something of value to them. Example: Using what you have that someone wants, like a guitar to get them to do something.

Legitimate power- Based on the user's position power. Example: As band leader members have to listen and do what you say. You are the one who can make decisions.

Referent power- Based on the user's personal power. Example: People will do things because of you, help you move, but won't do it for anybody else.

Information power- Based on the user's information being desired by others. Example: You have information to help other musicians and bands; if you don't share that information it could hurt or help them. They have to rely on you that will give you the power.

Expert power- Based on the user's skill and knowledge. Example: You are a skilled guitar player and publisher. Your skills and knowledge allow you to teach others. People can come to you for advice.

CHAPTER 8

HOW TO GENERATE INTEREST FROM THE PRESS

You can generate interest from the press by sending them a press release about anything that you feel is news worthy. Your press release can fall under the category of a human-interest story or entertainment. The following are some topics that could generate interest from the press:

- A new CD being released
- A CD release party
- A high profile or prestigious performance
- Individual or band achievements
- Signing a recording contract with a major record label
- Signing a contract with a major book publisher
- Starting a new business
- Obtaining a prestigious job at a college or university
- Touching lives in a positive way
- Bringing major recording artists to town
- Being a productive and interesting individual
- Performing at community events or fundraisers for a worthy cause

WRITING A PRESS RELEASE

Business Management for the Working Musician

When putting together your press release it is important to give it a headline. Be sure that the first sentence has a strong catchy phrase, something that will capture the reader's attention. It is also a nice touch to incorporate a quote from someone that is directly involved in the production.

A press release notifies the media about a particular story or event. It offers information such as, the type of event, the time and place of the event, ticket cost if any, where tickets can be purchased and any interesting background about the event. For example, who is involved and how did the event come to pass. A good press release should always include an e-mail address or website and a phone number for people to contact if they need further information. Janet Hawkins is the Associate Director of Public Affairs at Washtenaw Community College and this is what she has to say about writing a good press release.

> *There is a formula for writing a good press release. You want to put the who, what, where, when, why and how in the first paragraph. Expand on its details with the next paragraph. Provide background on the event our individual in the third paragraph. Have a call to action in the fourth paragraph. An ideal press release is one page, 1.5 spaced, and should introduce the news item to the reporter or editor. Remember that they're your audience. The first paragraph should pique their interest and the headline should summarize the news. We distribute most of our news items via email locally, so I dispense from the formal layout like the example attached. But if your students are going to learn how to structure a press release correctly, they should start with the basics.*

John E. Lawrence

IMPORTANT MEDIA TIPS FROM JANET HAWKINS

Establishing a personal relationship with the media is key to a successful promotional campaign. Musicians should know the people writing about music, that means reporters, bloggers and entertainment editors on a local, regional, and national scale.

Send them regular updates on performance times and venues, collaborations with other musicians, CD issues, and any other detail you think they might find interesting. With this kind of background, a reporter or blogger might incorporate you into a larger story without having to track you down for a comment, which can be problematic when you're on the road or in the studio.

Keep abreast of trends by reading the music columns and blogs regularly. What are they writing about? Technology in music? Emerging formats? Clubs that are up and coming or on their way out? What do you have to say about it?

Start a blog or website to showcase your activities and musicianship. Comment regularly on sites popular in your music genre or venue. But don't comment for comment's sake. You want to sound knowledgeable and engaged. Avoid using slang to project a polished image online or in an interview. Are you on Facebook? Twitter? Separate your personal from your professional persona on both--that means setting up separate account just for your music.

When preparing for an interview, anticipate the questions a reporter is likely to ask; and it is fine to ask what the article is about when setting up the interview. Prepare talking points or bullet key information you want to include in the discussion a head of time. The act of writing it down often cements it you're your consciousness and helps to avoid awkward moments. It's also a handy guide when you need a little reminder. You won't be able to anticipate every question but thinking about the story's theme and what you want to say a head of time about it will help you feel less nervous.

Last, but not least, network! Make sure your friends and family know what you're up to. Keep in contact with club owners, select reporters and former teachers. Let them know how to reach you if an opportunity comes their way. Good Luck!

The following examples are some actual press releases that were used for the Washtenaw Community College "Living Legends Award Series" and the "Sound Advice Lecture Series" written by Eleanor Shelton Writer/Editor Public Relations and Marketing.

John E. Lawrence

Public Relations and Marketing Services

Get Ready for The Temptations at WCC Dec. 14

ANN ARBOR, MI — Washtenaw Community College welcomes The Temptations Friday December 14 as part of the Living Legends Concert Series. The evening begins in Towsley Auditorium in the Morris Lawrence Building with an onstage interview at 7 p.m. followed by a full-length concert. Tickets are on sale now and are $75 for the first six rows; $55 for the rest of the main floor and $35 for the balcony.

This is the fifth year in a row that WCC has been able to attract luminary quality musicians to perform as part of the series.

"We are thrilled to have The Temptations perform at WCC," says John E. Lawrence, head of the Music Performance program and founder of the Living Legends Series. "This means so much to our students and our community that we get a chance to see them and learn about their musical challenges and triumphs. This concert series is special because the venue is intimate. The audience leaves feeling that they really got to know these musical legends."

The Music Performance program at WCC enrolls approximately 300 students who plan to make their career in music. From musicians to composers, engineers and producers, students leave the Music Performance program with the skills to get right to work to earn a living. Exposing WCC students to top caliber musicians and music professionals is part of the curriculum.

To learn more about the Living Legends Concert Series or to order your tickets visit www.wcclivinglegends.com or call (734) 973-3450.

Business Management for the Working Musician

Sound Advice for Emerging Musicians at WCC Dec. 1

ANN ARBOR, MI — Washtenaw Community College's Music Performance program offers *Sound Advice: Finding Success in the Era of New Media*, a free panel discussion December 1 in room 101 of the Morris Lawrence Building. The event is free and open to the public.

"With the poor economy there seem to be fewer and fewer live music venues. Musicians need to learn to use the benefits of social media sites like YouTube, Facebook and Myspace to generate a loyal fan base," says John E. Lawrence, head of the Music Performance program. We have four highly-regarded music producers all of whom have discovered their own best practices for using the Internet to build their own following or that of their clients."

The four panelists will be:

Luis Resto, Grammy award winning music producer who has worked with Madonna, Eminem and many others.

Sam Valenti, president of Ghostly Records and a leader in the Detroit Techno scene.

Chris Rizik, founder of SoulTracks.com the number one soul music web site in America.

Don Kline, Marketing Director for Fleming Artists, an agency representing some of the best touring musicians in the world.

The third in the yearly series, *Sound Advice* brings seasoned music professionals to emerging local musicians in an open environment. Some of the specific topics covered in this panel discussion are: Finding your niche; Identifying and reaching your audience; Promoting yourself; Using your audience as your street team; and Reaching record labels, media companies, and other music marketing avenues.

Reservations are recommended but not required. For more information or to make a reservation please call (734) 677-5146.

LETTING THE RIGHT PEOPLE KNOW THAT YOU ARE THERE

Someone once said, "If you want to move into a certain field you should get to know someone who is successful in that field." You should also let people know that you are available for work. Involve yourself with people who think the way you do and have the same interests. For example, if you are a dancer, you should get to know other dancers. If you are a musician, you should get to know other musicians. You should meet people that are grasping for the same goals. Surround yourself with positive reinforcements.

Remember, individuals that are not goal oriented may not agree with your vision and sometimes they will try to discourage you from following your dreams.

PUTTING TOGETHER A PRESS KIT

Promotional material for media: a packet of background and promotional material related to a product, distributed to the media by a publicist.

A press kit, often referred to as a media kit in business environments, is a prepackaged set of promotional materials of person, company, or organization distributed to members of the media.

A press kit is essential for generating interests from the media and establishing a relationship. This should include all of the items that will make it possible for the press to do a story about you.

Press kits are a common promotional tool used by musicians when launching a new CD. Band press kits often have their own unique set of components, including:

- Band biography/history of the band.

- Discography (all previous albums released by the band).

- Color selection of photos (many corporate photos are done in black and white for newspaper print purposes).

- CD and DVD.

- Past press coverage.

- A press release is telling the current news the media kit is sent in reference to.

- Contact information for the band's label, manager, publicist, the other representative quotes from others and contact information for those sources.

- Collateral advertising material, such as: postcard, flyer, newspaper ad, etc.

Many bands are utilizing the electronic press kit because it is easier to get it to the media and is easier for the media to respond via e-mail. The photographs and the printed material are sent electronically in a format that makes it easier for the media to use. Video footage of the band can also be included.

CREATE A MEDIA LIST

A media list is a list of all the local newspapers, magazines, news stations, and radio and TV stations. It also includes personnel and contact information. It will consist of their address, phone number, e-mail address and entertainment personnel (e.g., reporters, writers, editors, radio personalities etc.). This is a very important list because the individuals on this list can assist you with publicizing your event. Get to know them if possible and make sure that they know the quality of your work. When you contact them they will respond favorably?

PROMOTION: HOW AND WHEN TO PROMOTE

All newspapers and magazines have a deadline in which to submit a press release. Most of the monthly local papers and magazines have a deadline for all submissions to be in by the 10th day of the previous month. The press release would appear in the following month's issue. Most of the papers and magazines are issued to the newsstands and stores by the 1st of each month. If you would like to maximize your advertising time, try to schedule your events during the third or fourth week of the month. If you schedule your event during the first week of the month, people may not have enough time to read about it and plan to attend it.

POSTERS, FLYERS, AND TV

Posters and flyers are still a very effective way of getting the word out about your event. I like using posters and flyers because they can reach an audience that may not have a computer, read the newspaper, listen to the radio or watch TV. I believe in using all tools available to communicate an upcoming event. I don't want anyone to miss one of my events because they were not aware of it. I would prefer for them to say that they heard about it, but just could not make it. That way I am aware that my advertising campaign is working.

Posters and flyers can also be circulated by e-mail as a quick and easy way to reach hundreds of people. With everyone that you send the advertisement to, ask them to pass it along to everyone on their e-mail list.

Another form of advertising that I have tried is in the movie theater. Many cinema complexes have multiples theaters. Each one will show a slide of your poster multiple times before each movie. That means that your poster will be seen several times a day. I use this type of advertisement two weeks prior to the event. I like this type of advertisement because when people are seated in the movie theater waiting for the movie to start, they have no choice but to watch the movie screen.

Another way of advertising your event is to contact one of the local TV stations to request to be interviewed and maybe even do a short performance prior to the event. Some of them have a special spotlight section of the telecast where they feature local and national artists that are performing in the area.

Most cities have a public access television station, which promotes community events as well as host local TV shows. I found this to be an effective way to advertise my events. I go on the TV show as a special guest artist, do an interview and perform. This gives people an idea of what is in store for them the night of the show. Remember when you're being interviewed, to give out all of the pertinent information about your event: talk about what the event is, the events location, the date and time of the event and ticket information. Have the producer of the show; put together a slide with all of the information so they can be displayed on the screen as you speak.

CREATE A MAILING LIST

A mailing list is a list of all of your fans, people who enjoy watching you perform and listening to your music. A mailing list is important because you can notify people when you are performing in the area or when you have a new product to sell. This is how you can begin building your mailing list. Make cards for people to fill out with their name and contact information and distribute them at all of your performances.

Work to build your mailing list to 5000 people and notify them every time you have a performance. When you can tell a club owner or a concert promoter that you have 5000 people on your mailing list and guarantee a packed house everywhere you perform, it will separate you from the average band. Concert promoters, club owners, and even record labels will be interested in working with you.

THE MARKET ANALYSIS

In order to conduct a market analysis, you will have to do research, conduct studies and send out questionnaires and have them available for your audiences at your performances. The following are questions for the musician, entertainer or band who want to take their careers to the next level.

Find the answers to the following questions:

- How many people want to hear your music? Be Realistic. Test it.

- Who are your customers?

- What do they want?

- How much will they pay?

- How do you keep them coming back?

- How far does your fan base span and how can you expand it?

There are many musicians, entertainers and bands that never attain their maximum worth because they are under estimating their true value. They don't realize how much they are in demand.

Business Management for the Working Musician

Guitarist	Quantity	Income Per Unit	Weekly Hours	Weekly Income	Monthly Income	Yearly Income
Teacher/Private Lessons						
Home - Friday	6	$25.00 a student per 1/2 hr.	3 hours per week	$150.00	$600.00	$7,200.00
Music Stores – Saturday						
Performances						
Band Friday & Saturday/Parties/Clubs	1	$100 per performance	4 hours per week	$100.00	$400.00	$4,800.00
Recording Artist						
CD Sales	7	$15.00 each	7 CD s sold per week	$105.00	$420.00	$5,040.00
Studio Owner						
Studio Time	4	$25.00 per hr.	4hr. Recording Sessions a week	$100.00	$400.00	$4,800.00
						Total
						$21,840.00

A Sample Business Plan

John E. Lawrence

Guitarist	Quantity	Income Per Unit	Weekly Hours	Weekly Income	Monthly Income	Yearly Income
Teacher/Private Lessons and Instructor						
Home - Friday	10	$50.00 a student per 1/2 hr.	10 Students	$500.00	$2,000.00	$24,000.00
High Schools - Tuesday & Thursday	2	$35.00 per hr.	2 2hr. Classes	$140.00	$560.00	$6,720.00
Music Stores – Saturday	10	$40.00 a student per 1/2 hr.	10 Students	$400.00	$1,600.00	$19,200.00
Colleges - Monday & Wednesday (Part Time)	2	$45.00 per hr.	2 2hr. Classes	$180.00	$720.00	$8,640.00
Colleges - Monday through Thursday (Full Time)	9	$110.00 per hr.	16 hrs. per week	$1,758.75	$7,035.00	$84,420.00
Performances						
Solo Guitar Hotels/Restaurants/Club/Parties	2	$200.00 per performance	2 hrs twice a week	$400.00	$1,600.00	$19,200.00
Band Friday & Saturday/Parties/Clubs	2	$750.00 per performance $250 Band leader fee	4 hrs twice a week	$500.00	$2,000.00	$24,000.00
Churches Sunday	3	$150.00 per service	2 services once a week	$300.00	$900.00	$10,800.00
Booking Agent	5	15% of $750.00 = $112.50 X 5 Bands = $562.50	5 Artist once a month	$112.50	$450.00	$5,400.00
Concert Promoter	2	$30,000 per Concert	2 Major Concerts a Year	N/A	N/A	$60,000.00
Recording Artist						
CD Sales	10	$15.00 each	10 CD s sold per week @ $15.00 a CD	$150.00	$600.00	$7,200.00
DVD Sales	10	$25.00 each	10 DVD s sold per week @ $25.00 a DVD	$250.00	$1,000.00	$12,000.00
Owner of Super Trax Recording Company						
Studio Time	3	$35.00 per hr. X 4hrs = $140.00	3 4hr. Recording Sessions a week	$420.00	$1,680.00	$20,160.00
Studio Musician	3	$35.00 per hr. X 2hrs =$70.00	3 2hr. Recording Sessions a week	$210.00	$840.00	$10,800.00
Author/Royalties						
Chord Melody Solos	95	$1.00 each	95 Books sold per Quarter	$95.00	N/A	$380.00
Walking Bass Solos	95	$1.00 each	95 Books sold per Quarter	$95.00	N/A	$380.00
Improvising Solos	50	$1.00 each	50 Books sold per Quarter	$50.00	N/A	$200.00
Self-Management	40	$25.00 each	20 Books sold a Semester (Fall & Winter)	$1,000.00	N/A	$1,000.00
Endorsements						
Heritage Guitars (60% off)						
Takamine Guitars (50% off)						Total
LeBella Guitar Strings (free)						$314,500.00

CHAPTER 9

UTILIZING THE INTERNET

There are a lot of changes that have taken place in the music industry since the invention of the Internet. Some changes have been good for the industry, but others have hurt the industry. Some of the changes have leveled the playing field between the major record labels and the smaller independent ones. Even artists that produce and manufacture their own CD's now have the same capability to reach people as the major labels do. The Internet can be used as a virtual promotional pack to market artists, set up tours, and sell products worldwide.

Another change that has occurred is that people are not purchasing CD's in the way that they used to. Instead of going to the music store to purchase CD's, they purchase them from the Internet. People can also download music for free, which has drastically affected CD sales. They not only download free music, but they share it with their friends. Since most major labels don't make a huge profit on the sale of CD's any longer, they manufacture CD's for promotional use only.

Recording artists are now selling thousands of recordings without them being played on the radio. One of the advantages of being signed to a major record label was they could get you airplay nationwide. When your song became a hit, you would travel the country performing concerts. Radio used to be the only way people could find out about new artists or a new song. With the Internet, it is possible to become a national artist that tours worldwide and performs in front of an audience that is familiar with their material via the Internet.

YOUTUBE

YouTube enables artists to post the videos of their performances for the entire world to view. Not only can they view the performance, they can rate and critique it. This offers valuable information to an artist who wants to fine-tune their act before taking it out on the road. YouTube can also be used as a means of exposing artists globally to booking agents, club owners, concert promoters and TV.

MY SPACE

My Space offers the recording artist a chance to develop and build a fan base all over the world. A fan can spread the word about new recordings, about concert tours, and artist can even test out new material and get valuable feedback on what songs should be released. Some artists actually send out one or two songs free of charge to everyone connected to their Myspace page. They ask them to rate the song, give any type of feedback and share it with their friends for the purpose of building a fan base worldwide. For the first time, the consumer can have input in what they would like their favorite artist to release. This is something that has never been made possible before.

TWITTER

With the avenue of Twitter, a recording artist can keep in touch with their fans and give them daily updates on their career, products, and their personal lives. Imagine, before the Internet, being able to keep in contact with your favorite recording artist or band and have them communicate with you on a daily basis. Twitter is a connection between the recording artists and their fans. Fans can spread the word to their friends and family about the latest news they are receiving directly from the artist.

CHAPTER 10

PUTTING TOGETHER A PRACTICAL BUSINESS PLAN

Examine your daily schedule and figure out how much time can be devoted to your business. If you are a full-time student, you must take into consideration that your class schedule and study time will have a direct impact on how much time you spend developing your business. If you have a full or part-time job you must consider your work schedule as well. You must also consider that you are just starting your business and it will take some time to get it up and running.

- If your primary skill is being a musician and you want to perform, you must ask yourself realistically, how many performances you can do per week and how much are you going to charge. Just starting out, a realistic goal is to perform once a week at $100 per performance. Multiply that by four and that comes to $400 per month. Multiply $400 by 12 months and this will give you your projected yearly income (i.e. $4,800). Follow the same steps for each of the other related jobs or skills that you have.

- If your secondary skill is teaching and you devote two days a week to giving private lessons @$25 per half an hour, and you have six students, that averages out to $150 per week. Multiply by four weeks and that equals $600 per month. For 12 months, that equals $7,200 per year.

- If you own your own recording equipment then you can rent studio time. You can charge $25 per hour and you average one four hour recording session per week, which comes to $100 per week multiplied by four weeks in a month equals $400 per month multiplied by 12 months equals $4800 dollars per year.

- Since you own and operate your own recording studio, you can record and produce your own CDs and sell them for $15 each. If you sold one CD per day at $15 per CD that comes to $105 multiplied by four weeks equals $420 per month multiplied by 12 months equals $5040 per year. If you total it all together it comes to $21,840. That is not bad for a supplemental income.

It is important to note how many hours per week you are devoting to each job.

- Four hours per week for a four-hour performance.
- Six students at one half hour each equals three hours per week.
- one for our recording session per week equals four hours per week.
- CD Internet sales, music stores, performances and daily travels (no extra time required).

The total time spent for supplemental income per week is eleven hours per week.

Most full-time jobs require eight hours per day, which comes to 40 hours per week.

The self-employed artist can earn as much money as some who work conventional jobs, but it takes less time to earn it. We can increase our income by simply increasing the amount of time we spend per week working our craft or we can increase the cost for our services.

ESTABLISHING MULTIPLE SOURCES OF INCOME

Sample Business Plan:

- Performances: $100 per week equals $400 per month, which comes to $4800 per year.
- Private lessons: $150 per week equals $600 per month equals $7200 per year

- Recording sessions: $100 per week equals $400 per month equals $4800 per year
- CD sales: one CD sale per day at $15 each equals hundred and five dollars per week equals $420 per month equals $5040 per year
- Total yearly income: $21,840

If you are earning $21,840 per year working in the hours per week and you can double your workload to twenty-two hours per week and double your income to $43,680 annually and that's only half of time a person spends working full time at a conventional job. An added bonus is that you are doing something that you enjoy.

I advise working a conventional job and consider the work that you do as an artist as supplemental income. Work this way until you are earning just as money much or more than your conventional job pays, then you can continue to work both jobs or that the conventional job go and work your craft full-time. A full-time artist can double their annual income of $43,680 by working 44 hours per week instead of 22 hours, which brings their annual yearly income to $87,360. Remember this is based on a person that utilizes four of their artistic goals only. Most people will discover that they can work even more hours, which increases their income even more.

FROM BEING AN EMPLOYEE TO BEING AN EMPLOYER

Career Planning: now, next year, 10 years out, middle age, end of career.

Some employees have the mindset that they are supposed to try to do the minimum amount of work for the maximum pay. I first experienced this in the days of working as a busboy when I was in my teens. The second time I experienced this type of thinking was when I worked at an automotive factory in my twenties. The difference was that the autoworkers were serious about trying to look busy while doing a minimal amount of work. Their goal was to attract the least amount attention to themselves while doing their job.

John E. Lawrence

I can recall the first day I was hired in as a factory worker. I wanted to show the foreman and my coworkers that I was a good worker. My production was at least twice as much as everyone else's. Then a coworker came to me and said, "you are working too hard and too fast". I smiled and took it as a compliment and continue to work just as hard. After ten or fifteen minutes, he returned and said, "slow down!" This time he was not smiling. He went on to say that the workers in the factory has spent many years convincing the higher ups who had been trying to get them to increase production that it could not be done and that they are performing at the optimal performance level. He went on to say that if I continued to work at such a fast paced that it will show the bosses that we can up production and they would expect everyone to work equally as fast, so slow the ____ down! I realized that I was quickly making enemies, so I slowed down my production.

Even in the world of academia you will find teachers and college instructors who would do just enough to get by and nothing more. They are masters at doing the minimum amount of work in receiving the maximum amount of pay. They have their job security and they are literally coasting to retirement.

This kind of thinking does not work to your advantage when you own your own business. You must change your mind set to think like an employer instead of an employee. You must work long hours because if you do not do the necessary work to make your business succeed no one else will do it for you. If you take pride in your work and your goal is to deliver quality than you would not mind going the extra mile.

Dr. Morris J. Lawrence Jr., who was the driving force behind Washtenaw Community College's Performing Arts Department for years, used to tell his music students that they should give 110 % every time they take their instrument out of the case to play it, and if you are not willing to do that they do not even bother taking your instrument out of the case.

VIEW YOURSELF AS A BUSINESS

View yourself as a business. What does it mean to view you as a business? First, we must define the word business. The Encarta Dictionary gives this definition:

- A line of work

- A particular trade or profession.

- The retail business

- Commercial organization or company or other organization that buys and sells goods, makes products, or provides services.

- Commercial activity involving the exchange of money for goods or services.

- Something excellent

Let's recap what it means to be a business. A business person is someone in a particular trade or profession who buys and sells goods. They make products or provides services involving the exchange of money.

When I think of what artists do as creative individuals and compare it to the above definition of a business, I have come to the realization that "We Are the Business."

- Think about the recording artist who produces and sales CDs. This coincides with definitions two and four.

- The studio engineer charges the client for the use of their studio and services. This aligns with definition number two.

- Definition number four could also be related to a band that exchanges money for their performances.

- An artist creates a product (artwork) in exchange for money.

- A teacher offers their knowledge and expertise as a product in exchange for money.

- The success of the above professions aligns with number one and number five; there are lines of work and you must deliver excellence.

Before I move to the next topic, I would like to leave you with one thought. "Be the business and work your business". Be business minded and think of yourself as business owners and provide quality service. We are the owner and sole proprietor of the small business.

The next step is to make it legal by filing necessary paperwork with The County Register's Office. The Form Is Called an Assumed Name form a DBA form which stands for "Doing Business As"

"We Are the Business"

John E. Lawrence__

The following is an example of an Assumed Name form. Once the form is filled out, it should be registered with the County Clerk/Registers office.

M.C.L.A. 445.1 et seq.
M.C.L.A. 445.2B
FILING FEE $10.00

LAWRENCE KESTENBAUM
WASHTENAW COUNTY CLERK/REGISTER

THIS IS A LEGAL DOCUMENT
TYPE OR PRINT CLEARLY
USE BLACK OR BLUE INK

REMIT PAYMENT / MAIL TO:
WASHTENAW COUNTY CLERK
200 N. MAIN ST., SUITE 100, P.O. BOX 8645
ANN ARBOR, MI 48107-8645
TELEPHONE (734) 222-6720

WASHTENAW COUNTY — CERTIFICATE OF ASSUMED NAME
THIS CERTIFICATE EXPIRES FIVE (5) YEARS FROM THE DATE OF FILING

THE UNDERSIGNED, hereby certifies that the following persons now owns (or) intends to own, conduct or transact business in the County of Washtenaw, State of Michigan, under the designation, name or style stated below:

1. AN ORIGINAL_____ RENEWAL_____ CHANGE OF LOCATION_____ DISSOLUTION_____
2. NAME OF BUSINESS_____
3. PRINCIPAL ADDRESS OF BUSINESS_____
      number & street   city   state   zip code
4. (PRINT) FULL LEGAL NAME(S) OF PERSON(S)   RESIDENCE ADDRESS(ES)

   first   middle   last   number and street

                            city   state   zip code

   first   middle   last   number and street

                            city   state   zip code

5. NON-RESIDENTS OF MICHIGAN, MUST FILE A "CONSENT TO SERVICE" (BN-05). FILING FEE $2.00.
6. SIGNATURE(S) OF ALL PERSON(S) LISTED ABOVE — **MUST BE WITNESSED BY A NOTARY PUBLIC.**

(Signature)_____
(Signature)_____
(Notary Signature)_____

STATE OF MICHIGAN   } ss.
COUNTY OF WASHTENAW }

Subscribed and sworn to before me this

day, _____
    month   day   year

Printed Name_____
Notary Public, _____ County, MI
Acting In _____ County, MI
Commission expires_____

FOR OFFICE USE ONLY — DO NOT WRITE BELOW THIS LINE

Counter ☐   Mail ☐   Franchise   Yes ☐   No ☐   Approved _____ / _____

CERTIFICATION OF RECORD

STATE OF MICHIGAN } ss
COUNTY OF WASHTENAW }

I, LAWRENCE KESTENBAUM, CLERK/REGISTER OF SAID COUNTY OF WASHTENAW DO HEREBY CERTIFY that the foregoing is a true and exact copy of the original document on file in my office.

Dated: _____

Lawrence Kestenbaum

LAWRENCE KESTENBAUM,
WASHTENAW COUNTY CLERK/REGISTER

John E. Lawrence

SELF-EMPLOYMENT AND WHY IT IS THE BEST JOB SECURITY

In my opinion, working for yourself is the best career choice and why the entertainment industry is one of the best industries to work in with today's economy.

- When you work for yourself you never get fired or laid off. Another reason why working for yourself is a good idea is that if you need more money to cover your monthly expenditures, you can simply take on more clients in order to increase your income.

- If you are working for an employer, your monthly income is predetermined, and it does not matter how hard you work, you pay remains the same and if your pay does not meet your monthly expenditures then some of the bills will have to go unpaid.

- If you are a musician you can total up your monthly bills and figure out how many performances will have to be added to your monthly schedule or how many private students have been added in order to increase your income to the point that matches your monthly expenditures. Another option is to increase your rates.

- If you have multiple sources of income you can sell more CDs, books or studio time, sale jingles, take on more students and book more performances to generate more income. As an artist and a creative individual, you will always have options. You have to make things happen for you and not let things happen to you.

Times are changing, and you must either change with the times or be left behind. There was a time when if a person landed the job in the auto industry they were set for life. They received high wages, good benefits and as much over time as they could handle. I never would have imagined the jobs and the automobile industry would be disappearing at such an alarming rate. Hundreds of thousands of workers are out of work and it does not look like those jobs will ever return. Many of them are returning to college to gain knowledge that will enable them to move into a different field. Some are moving into skill trades.

Washtenaw Community College enrollment has increased by 20% over the two academic years 2008 and 2009. The increase is largely due to the fact that people are recognizing that the job market has changed, and they have to change with it or be left behind.

The bottom has dropped out of the real estate market. Thousands of people are losing their houses to foreclosure because they can no longer afford their house payments. Some people are faced with the fact that property values have dropped to the point that they owe more money on their house than what it is worth. Some people owe as much as two times the value of their home, which means they cannot even sale their home to get out from under the house payment. This is why some people are going to the bank and handing over their house keys and simply walking away. It would be cheaper for them to purchase a house in today's market than to continue paying on their existing mortgage.

If a person purchased a house for $300,000 house five years ago that same house is now worth $150,000 in today's market. It is known as being upside down in your mortgage. As little as ten years ago, a person could purchase a house for $150,000 and within a few years that same house would be worth $300,000. They would have accumulated $150,000 in equity. They could then sell their house and walk away with $150,000 cash; not a bad return on their investment.

MAKING MONEY DURING HARD ECONOMIC TIMES

There are still plenty of businesses that are thriving through these hard economic times. They are known as "Recession Proof Businesses". Some people are making more money now than they ever have in their life.

The following is a list of the top ten recession proof industries:

- Healthcare

- Federal government

- Skilled services

- Food manufacturing

- Alternative energy

- Career services

- Big-box retailers like Wal-Mart and Costco

- Accounting

- Movie and entertainment industry

- Education

This is a prime time for people to stop and take a look around and look at their options. You must understand that it will take a new way of thinking a new way of operating your business, new concepts and changing with the times. Be flexible and keep your options open and be willing to change if necessary. Just because you started out on one path, does not mean that is the only path you should take.

There is plenty of room for the person that has an entrepreneur spirit and is willing to take risks to meet the needs of the consumer. Someone once said, "Always invest in things that people need."

CHAPTER 11

Avoid putting obstacles in your way

It is difficult enough to be successful in this world, so do not develop habits that will deplete your income once you become financially secure or while you are on your way to becoming financially secure. I am a firm believer that people should avoid doing things that will cause them to spend money unnecessarily. Don't misunderstand, I am not saying that you do not deserve to have the finer things in life. I believe that people should be able to do more than just pay their bills and simply exist. One of the advantages of being financially secure is that you can purchase the things that you desire, as well as, the things that you need in order to survive.

There are some things that people bring upon themselves that prevent them from living the lifestyle that they desire and deserve. I call them the "Terrible Ings". You would be surprised at how much money people throw away weekly on things like:

- Gambling
- Drinking
- Smoking
- Drugs
- Over eating

THE FIVE MOST EXPENSIVE ADDICTIONS

Despite the growing publicity about "soft" addictions, drinking, smoking, drug abuse, over eating, and gambling still are the costliest to society. There has been a study that proves that the typical person spends $15,000 a year on his or her soft addictions, and no one has ever spent less than $3000.

Alcohol. Estimated annual cost: $166 billion. Binge drinking hits the unemployed harder on a per capita basis -- 10.4%, vs. 8.4% of employed people. It is most prevalent in small metropolitan locales, rather than big cities or rural areas. The $18 billion spent on alcohol and drug treatment last year represented 1.3% of all health care spending.

Smoking. Estimated annual cost: $157 billion. The tab includes $75 billion in direct medical expenses, with the rest in lost productivity from ill patients missing work. Given the low-tax (or no-tax) underground cigarette economy on the Web and on Indian reservations, it's unlikely that sales and usage have dropped much over the past decade, official government statistics notwithstanding.

Drugs. Estimated annual cost: $110 billion. Like alcohol, illicit drug use is more prevalent among the unemployed. Most addicts are also heavy drinkers, though only small minorities of alcoholics are drug abusers. Crystal meth has followed marijuana, cocaine, and heroin as the drug of choice.

Overeating. Estimated annual cost: $107 billion. Overeating increases the risk of many health problems, including heart attacks. Obesity causes 14% of attacks suffered by males and 20% of those suffered by females, the National Institutes for Health says, and less than a third of adults get regular exercise. The bulk of the $107 billion is the direct cost to treat heart disease, osteoarthritis, hypertension, gall bladder disease and cancer.

Gambling. Estimated annual cost: $40 billion. Addicted gamblers often feel compelled to chase after bad bets with more money in the hope of winning back their losses. And some who catch the fever develop the need to periodically raise the betting stakes to keep the same thrill. Also, addicts often face job loss, bankruptcy and forced home sales, and they are at greater risk to commit crimes like forgery and embezzlement.

CHOOSING THE RIGHT MATE

I don't think there has been enough dialogue of this subject among artists. It is probably because it is such a delicate and personal topic. It is still very important and should be addressed, because finding the right mate can inspire you to strive and push yourself further than you could have ever imagined. On the other hand, finding the wrong mate can stunt your growth as an artist and a creative person. It can ruin your career before it gets started. I would like to share with you some situations that I have encountered.

I knew of two female keyboard players who were very talented. I really wanted to work with them both, but it never came to pass. They would do things such as not showing up for rehearsals and recording sessions. Sometimes, they would even turn down performance opportunities. I had to stop using them because of their inability to make a commitment. Later I found out that they were married to men who were extremely jealous. Their husbands would make their lives miserable when they found out they were performing with a man. They would cancel rehearsals and turn down performances in order to keep the peace at home.

Another situation I encountered was with one of my guitar students. He was one of my top of my top students. He would always do his homework assignments and showed a lot of potential. I expected him to go far with this music studies and his musical career. About halfway through the semester, I noticed that he would show up to class unprepared and then he began missing quite often.

Being concerned, I had a talk with him after class one day to find out what was wrong. He told me that he had a new girlfriend and she wanted him to spend his free time with her. I explained to him that there is nothing wrong with spending time together, as long as it doesn't interfere with your studies and goals in life. He also said, that whenever he would practice his guitar and she was around, she would say things like "you like your guitar more than me." In order to keep her happy, he wouldn't practice. As a result, he almost failed the class. If he had continued studying and practicing as he did at the beginning of the semester, he would have received an "A" in the class.

I may not be an expert on relationships, but if you have to give up your dreams in order to make someone else happy, then that is not a healthy relationship. I might not be able to tell you how to find the right mate but, I can tell you how to recognize the wrong one. If you meet someone that wants to stop you from doing the things that bring you joy and happiness, then you are with the wrong mate.

There is an R&B singing group by the name of "The Impressions" that was popular in the 60s 70s and 80s that recorded a song entitled "The Same Thing It Took" to chorus to the song says; "The same thing it took to get your baby hooked, just going to take the same thing to keep her."

My advice to finding the right mate is to continue doing the things that you enjoy, and you will attract people with similar interests. They will notice and appreciate your skill, talent and passion for what you do and gravitate towards you. I believe that you have to be happy and content with who you are in order to make someone else happy.

CHAPTER 12

THE IMPORTANCE OF ESTABLISHING GOOD CREDIT

There is another mistake that people make that will put out of obstacles in their way from the start and they can prevent them from being able to acquire the basic essentials of life. They can make banks and other loan institutions consider you a bad risk. You will be unable to acquire loans that can be useful when it comes to starting a business, purchasing equipment, an automobile or a house. The mistake that people make is either not paying their bills on time or not paying them at all. This damages your credit report and lowers your credit rating.

This is especially important to young people just starting to build their credit. It is important because they are starting with a clean slate. If you have a good credit rating you will be able to purchase the major items like a house or car without any problems. Put yourself in the position that will enable you to make these types of purchases without the need of a cosigner.

AVOID THE CREDIT CARD TRAP

Credit card companies make purchasing items sound good by offering you the chance to purchase now and pay later. You can even make payments on your purchases a little time, by making the minimum payment. A person can purchase thousands of dollars' worth of merchandise and their monthly minimum payment might be less than $100.

This sounds good, but what you may not realize is that if a person pays the minimum payment on a credit card each month you are only paying the interest costs and the principle of balance that people on the credit card remains the same on some cases will increase. It depends on the annual percentage rate on your credit card.

Some credit cards come with an APR of 18 to 25%. This makes it impossible to pay off the card is then make the minimum payment. Some people will purchase enough items that they reach the limit that the credit card will allow, so they acquired more credit cards. Since they have been paying the minimum payment on the previous credit card credit card companies look at them as to the customers and they will increase your credit limit.

Understand that when a credit card company increases your credit limit does not mean you are improving your overall credit rating or score. The average American has eight credit cards and is about $8000 in debt.

HOW TO GET OUT OF CREDIT CARD DEBT

The following strategies can help you get of credit card debt:

- Always pay more than the minimum payment due each month. Because when you pay the minimum payment it only covers the interest owed. In some cases your debt will actually increase when you pay the minimum payment.

- Pay extra money toward the principal whenever possible because, most of your payment goes toward interest.

- Some credit card companies will offer a special introductory rate of 0% interest for six months on all balance transfers. You use this as a means to pay additional and eventually get out of debt. This is the home of works.

- Apply for the 0% interest rate credit card, then transfer the balance from of your high interest rate credit cards to the new 0% interest rate credit card. Remember to mark on the calendar the date that

- The introductory rate will end. About two to three weeks before the offer ends, sign up for another 0% interest rate credit card and transfer the entire balance from the previous credit card to the new one. If you have been paying money toward the additional principal than the balance that is transferred will be less.

- Repeat this process over and over until you have a zero balance on your credit card.

- Then cancel the credit card and cut it up or shred. This is a way of removing the temptation to use the credit card and prevent you from ever falling into the credit card trap again.

KEEP GOOD TAX RECORDS

After you have filled out your DBA (Doing Business As) or your Assumed Name Certificate you can take it to a bank and open up a business account in the name of your business. The bank will supply you with all of the information necessary for you to order business checks and deposit slips in the name of your business.

Once you have the business account open, you should have your clients that pay with a check make the check payable to the name of your business. Deposit the check into your business account and then pay your employees or band members with a business check. Even the owner of the business should be paid with a business check. The reason is so you can keep good track of the income and expenses that are generated from the business. It is important to keep the income from other sources separate from the business, that way you can monitor the revenue from the business and see exactly how the business is doing. All purchases for the business should be paid with a business check.

Every employee who is paid $600 or more from January 1 to December 31, of the same year has to be issued a 1099 tax form. The 1099 tax form is a form that shows the income of each employee or band member and they must pay taxes on the earned income to Internal Revenue Service (IRS). The employer must file the appropriate form alerting the IRS that the 1099 tax forms have been sent to the employees.

WORKING CORPORATE ENGAGEMENTS

Some corporate engagements will require you to send them an invoice prior to the engagement over for them to issue you a paycheck. Some institutions such as colleges and universities require you to render the service before they can begin processing the paperwork for you to receive your paycheck. This means that your check will not be available the night of the performance. Do not worry; this is standard procedure.

BEING A PROFESSIONAL ON AND OFF THE STAGE

There are some computer software programs that can assist you in your business operations. The software that I prefer is: Quick Books Pro. It is manufactured by Intuit. It is business financial software that will help you to organize your business and save time tracking your finances. It makes you look more professional. The software will:

- Print checks, pay bills and track expenses
- Track sales, sales tax and customer payments
- Manage payroll and payroll taxes
- Create professional-looking invoices and forms
- E-mail estimates, invoices, reports, and more
- Organize and backup documents by attaching them to your Quick Books records
- Accept credit cards and debit cards right in QuickBooks

Get insight so you can make better decisions:

- One-click business reports

- Track inventory, set reorder points and create purchase orders

- Get an immediate view into your bottom line all in one page with company snapshot

- Easily create a business plan

- Forecast sales and expenses

The more together and professional your business looks to your clients, the more trust they will have when it comes to hiring your services. If a client has trust in your business, they will not have a problem recommending you to other potential clients. About 90% of my business comes through referrals of satisfied customers.

John E. Lawrence

CHAPTER 13

DEVELOPING AND PRODUCING A PRODUCT

The following are some steps one should consider when making a CD.

Start working on gathering the material that will be on the project. This can involve deciding on a theme for the CD some themes are: dance, jazz, love, protest, rock, high-energy, mellow, message, groove, anger, or any of life's emotions, situations, and feelings etc. the songs can be original material or written by someone else or you may want to find someone that you can work with and do a collaboration. Some artists choose to record remakes of popular songs that have been previously released and some go for the more obscure songs and give them new life.

If you are planning on recording 10 songs for the CD, then it will be a good idea for you to record 15 songs and choose the 10 best songs. Before you start recording is a good idea to find a producer for the project. Some artists choose to self-produce their musical projects and do a good job with the production.

This is the Wikipedia definition of the word "producer:"

A record producer is an individual working within the music industry, whose job is to oversee and manage the production of an artist's music. The producer has many roles that include, but are not limited to, coaching the musicians, controlling the recording sessions, gathering the ideas of the product, and supervising the final production through mixing and mastering. Over the latter half of the 20th century, producers have also taken on a wider entrepreneurial role, with responsibility for budget, schedules, and negotiations.

Today, the recording industries have two kinds of producers: executive producer and music producer; they have different roles. While the executive producer has the financial role of the project, the music producer is responsible for the music of an album.

The music producer could, in some cases, be compared to the film director in that the producer's job is to create, shape and mold a piece of music in accordance with their vision for the album.

Next up is to find musicians to work on the project rehearsed them until they are ready to go into the recording studio. Find a good recording studio that meets your needs. Some studios are set up for basically a one-man operation and others are equipped with the space and equipment to record all of the musicians at the same time. The recording studio is not a place for rehearsals because you're paying by the hour and time is money so make sure that everyone is well prepared and familiar with the music before you go into the recording studio to start laying tracks.

After all the tracks have been recorded, the next stage is the mixing sessions. The mixing process involves the blending of all of the recorded tracks. This is what is known as "signal processing." The sound of an instrument or voice can be altered by changing the equalization, the volume and by adding effects such as: reverb, (determines the size of the room of the instrument during playback) digital delay, (stores sound in space and releases it at a predetermined time.) Compression compresses the sound being played back. Some artists will mix a song as many as 15 to 20 times before they settle on a final mix. The goal is to get the music so that it meets industry standards and is ready to be sold and played right next to the songs that are heard on the radio daily, this is what is known as being "radio ready."

DIFFERENT PROFESSIONAL BRANCHES

There are four distinct steps to commercial production of a recording: Recording, editing, mixing, and mastering. Typically, a sound engineer who specializes only in that part of production performs each.

1. A studio engineer could be either a sound engineer working in a studio together with a producer, or a producing sound engineer working in a studio.

2. A recording engineer is a person who records sound.

3. A mixing engineer is a person who creates mixes of multi-track recordings. It is not uncommon for a commercial record to be recorded at one studio and later mixed by different engineers in other studios.

4. A mastering engineer typically the person who mixes the final stereo tracks (or sometimes just a few tracks or stems) that the mix engineer produces. The mastering engineer makes any final adjustments to the overall sound of the record in the final step before commercial duplication. Mastering engineers use principles of equalization and compression to affect the coloration of the sound.

The next step is photography and CD cover design.

To better explain the process of designing a CD cover, I have called upon Michael Tanner. He is the graphic designer who designed all of my CD covers. This is what Michael has to say.

ADVICE FROM GRAPHIC DESIGNER MICHAEL TANNER

My name is Michael P. Tanner and I have been a graphic designer for 26 years. I have been designing music and video packaging for World Class Tapes of Ann Arbor, Michigan. I started working at WCT in 1997 and at that time cassette on shell design and packaging was what we did most. However, over the years CD replication has replaced cassette duplication and I shifted my work to CD packaging design. DVD video package has also replaced VHS tapes as the medium of choice for video production.

Throughout my time here at WCT I have worked closely with many musicians from all over the USA and other countries as well. Sitting down with a client is the best way for me to develop a good idea as to what the project is all about and what direction the client would like the design to go. This aspect of the way I design differs quite a bit from most artists who work on the ideas independent of their clients. Some come in with everything worked out in great detail (or completed, in which case all I do in check that the job is in the correct template and will work properly for our printers) other clients come in with no idea or direction to go. These clients are the hardest to get started but as with all of the projects that I have worked on, once I get started it just take shape all on its own.

The first question I ask the client is what kind of music is desired. This is important because it try to match the image that will be used for the CD cover to the music. If there is a photograph or an image that the client wants to work with, I will start there. Then I will insert the title of the CD, on the photograph. The most difficult part of the job is to pick a font (type face) that works with the overall mood of the project.

After the cover is set the rest of the project comes together pretty quickly. The next step is to layout whatever is included in the rest of the booklet including lyrics of the song, special thanks, production information, and any images that work with the overall design.

When the booklet is complete I move on the tray card; this is the piece of printed paper that belongs under the tray that will hold the CD itself, it also includes the spines on the ends. This part can be tricky because of the amount of information that a lot of clients want here, song list, contact info, barcode, and copyright information.

The next step is designing the CD label. This is a little different because it does not start with a white piece of paper as a printing surface, it is the silver reflective surface of the disc itself. This extra element can make for a very exciting design. Discs are usually designed in solid color from the Pantone Color Matching System. However; with improvements in disc printing technology full color disc are a better way to go in some cases. Discs are usually screen printed and this is why solid color work best. However, there is a new off-set disc printing system that has improved full color disc printing dynamically.

The following are examples of the CD covers that Michael Tanner has designed for me. I have included a CD description alongside of each CD, so you see the coalition of the CD design and the music on the CD.

CDS RECORDED AND PRODUCED BY JOHN E. LAWRENCE

John E. Lawrence

Old Smooth is a comprised of remakes of hit songs from the 60's 70's and 80's performed in a Smooth Jazz format. It includes songs like: "We're In This Love Together," "Say Yes," "Your Song," " The Tracks of My Tears" and more. This CD continues to be my best selling CD to date primarily because of the popularity of the material. Music has the power to take people back to the exact point and time when they first heard the song. This CD has sentimental value which is a feature that a CD that is made up of original material can not do.

Summer Nights John produced, engineered, arranged and played nearly every instrument on his CD. The songs on this CD fall into three jazz styles, Smooth jazz, Latin jazz and Cool Jazz. The CD contains twelve original compositions, plus a moving rendition of Michael Jackson's "Man In The Mirror." John put this CD together with three goals in mind: 1) This project has to display the type of playing excitement generated in his live performances; 2) Most of the songs must be original compositions and display a variety of styles; and 3) Every song has to have a strong melody. This thirteen-song collection is John's best work to date.

All By Myself is a solo guitar project. It features John E. Lawrence primarily on acoustic guitar performing with no other instruments and no overdubs. The CD highlights John's unique style of playing chords, melody, and walking bass lines simultaneously. He introduces a style he developed, called "Polyrhythmic Percussive Funk". This style utilizes the guitar as a percussion instrument as well as a melodic and rhythmic instrument. The songs that feature this style are Black Orpheus, "Birdland," and "I Wish." There are some beautiful ballads on this project: the title song, "All By Myself" (an original composition), "America the Beautiful" and "The Theme from M.A.S.H." This CD separates him from other guitarist and illustrates his mastery of the instrument.

Old Smooth is comprised of remakes of hit songs from the 60's 70's and 80's performed in a Smooth Jazz format. It includes songs like: "We're In This Love Together," "Say Yes," "Your Song," "The Tracks of My Tears" and more. This CD continues to be my best-selling CD to date primarily because of the popularity of the material. Music has the power to take people back to the exact point and time when they first heard the song. This CD has sentimental value which is a feature that a CD that is made up of original material cannot do.

All By Myself is a solo guitar project. It features John E. Lawrence primarily on acoustic guitar performing with no other instruments and no overdubs. The CD highlights John's unique style of playing chords, melody, and walking bass lines simultaneously. He introduces a style he developed, called "Polyrhythmic Percussive Funk". This style utilizes the guitar as a percussion instrument as well as a melodic and rhythmic instrument. The songs that feature this style are Black Orpheus, "Birdland," and "I Wish." There are some beautiful ballads on this project: the title song, "All By Myself" (an original composition), "America the Beautiful" and "The Theme from M.A.S.H." This CD separates him from other guitarists and illustrates his mastery of the instrument.

John E. Lawrence

Winter Wonderland is a CD that has put together made up of holiday favorites that are sure to bring in the Christmas joy. The project includes songs such as: "Jingle Bell Rock," and "Do You Hear What I Hear." Listen to classic jazz renditions of "Winter Wonderland" and "White Christmas." The guitar solos on "Jingle Bells" and the timeless classic " The Christmas Song" (Chestnuts) are simply breathtaking. The Winter Wonderland project is a CD that music lovers will be listening to for generations to come.

Merry Christmas from John E. Lawrence is a Christmas gift to all who enjoy the Christmas season. The CD starts off with a rockin' version of "God Rest Ye Merry Gentlemen" It is high-energy and is masterfully executed. John reached back into his childhood memories and brought back "The Chipmunk Christmas" and a song from the Charlie Brown Christmas special and put together an adult version of " Christmas Time is Here" which features a dynamic saxophone solo by his teacher and mentor, Dr. Morris J. Lawrence Jr.

A Solo Guitar Christmas is a CD for the guitar aficionado that enjoys an intimate listening experience with a guitar virtuoso. John performs two four song medlies of traditional Christmas music. Song titles include: "What Child Is This," "O' Tannenbaum," "My Favorite Things," "We Three Kings" and more... There are two bonus tracks, "Have Yourself a Merry Little Christmas" and a beautiful original composition entitled, I'll Remember Christmas.

Summer Nights: John produced, engineered, arranged and played nearly every instrument on his CD. The songs on this CD fall into three jazz styles, Smooth jazz, Latin jazz and Cool Jazz. The CD contains twelve original compositions, plus a moving rendition of Michael Jackson's "Man In The Mirror." John put this CD together with three goals in mind: 1) This project has to display the type of playing excitement generated in his live performances; 2) Most of the songs must be original compositions and display a variety of styles; and 3) Every song has to have a strong melody. This thirteen-song collection is John's best work to date.

Winter Wonderland is a CD that has put together made up of holiday favorites that are sure to bring in the Christmas joy. The project includes songs such as: "Jingle Bell Rock," and "Do You Hear What I Hear." Listen to classic jazz renditions of "Winter Wonderland" and "White Christmas."

The guitar solos on "Jingle Bells" and the timeless classic "The Christmas Song" are simply breathtaking. The Winter Wonderland project is a CD that music lovers will be listening to for generations to come.

Merry Christmas from John E. Lawrence is a Christmas gift to all who enjoy the Christmas season. The CD starts off with a rockin' version of "God Rest Ye Merry Gentlemen" It is high-energy and is masterfully executed.

John reached back into his childhood memories and brought back "The Chipmunk Christmas" and a song from the Charlie Brown Christmas special and put together an adult version of "Christmas Time is Here" which features a dynamic saxophone solo by his teacher and mentor, Dr. Morris J. Lawrence Jr.

A Solo Guitar Christmas is a CD for the guitar aficionado that enjoys an intimate listening experience with a guitar virtuoso. John performs two four-song medleys of traditional Christmas music. Song titles include: "What Child Is This," "O' Tannenbaum," "My Favorite Things," "We Three Kings" and more. There are two bonus tracks, "Have

John E. Lawrence

Yourself a Merry Little Christmas" and a beautiful original composition entitled, I'll Remember Christmas.

Information Found on the CD Cover and Insert

I decided to go with a four-panel insert on my "Summer Nights" CD and this is how we laid it out.

The front cover panel should display a photo that depicts mood or the style of music that is recorded on the project as well as the artist's name and the title of the CD. Some bands have such a unique name and image to where their name is representative a type of trademark and that trademark is displayed on all of their CD covers in different ways. Some bands that represent this type of marketing are: "Earth Wind and Fire" "Metallica" "MAZE Featuring Frankie Beverly" and "The Average White Band."

Below is a copy of my CD cover entitled "Summer Nights" The style of music on the CD is Contemporary Jazz, notice how the images, text and layout all tie into the theme of experiencing a Jazzy summer night out on the town.

The front rear cover panel is where I list things such as: executive producer, producers, recording studios, engineers, songwriters and booking information. I also utilized this panel to display another photo of myself playing my guitar in the moonlight.

John E. Lawrence

The inside fold panels display the order of the song titles and their length, guest musicians, arrangers, the type of equipment used on the project, photography, graphic designer, endorsements, and including a special thanks. I took this opportunity to include another photograph and reemphasize the protection rights on the music. Notice that the text is printed on photograph of the Renaissance Center in the city of Detroit MI at night for the background.

Some graphic designers recommend listening to the CD to inspire them to create images and an overall concept for the design of the CD Cover. It is also a good idea to go to a music store and take a look at how other recording artists CD cover design work is done in order to give you ideas. Remember that major record labels have a team of graphic designers whose job is to come up with creative CD cover designs for their recording artists and you can learn from them.

Business Management for the Working Musician

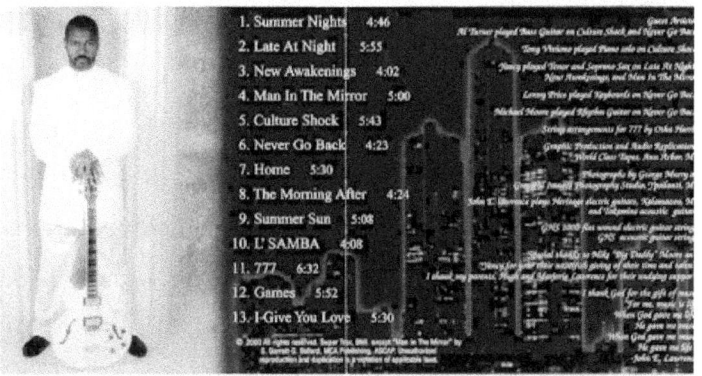

The back of the jewel case can be used to list song titles and the song order so people who are interested in purchasing CDs can read the contents without opening it. This is also a good place for listing your contact and booking information. Be sure to use contact information such as phone numbers and addresses that will usable for long periods of time. If your address is constantly changing people will not be able to contact you. So instead of using a temporary apartment address go to the United States Post Office and purchase a P.O. Box so even if you move, your address will still remain the same.

Most record companies utilize the back of the jewel case to advertise their record label and publishing company special guest recording artist or writers. Include copyright protection information and the unauthorized reproduction and duplication is a violation of applicable laws statement and the record label, band or artist logo. The back-of a CD is also the most common place to place a barcode.

Most retail outlets require that all items sold must have a barcode printed on it. A barcode is an optical machine-readable representation of data, which shows certain data on a certain product. A printed simple intended to be read by a computer, used for a variety of purposes, such as product identification at point-of-sale and tracking items in a warehouse.

John E. Lawrence

HOW I LANDED A BOOK PUBLISHING DEAL WITH MEL BAY PUBLICATIONS

Mel Bay Publications is a very prestigious American publishing company that specializes in publishing instructional material for musical instrument playing. It was found in 1947 by the guitarist and tenor banjo player Mel Bay (1913-1997) and is based in Pacific, Missouri.

It is an honor to be an author for Mel Bay publications because of their longevity and their reputation for publishing quality instructional books. Along with being associated with a publisher that has published thousands of books, Mel Bay holds a special place in my heart because as a young child I studied from Mel Bay's modern guitar method book volume and that book is still in print and being published to date.

This is my story.

I have recorded and published a solo guitar instructional videotape entitled "Jazz Improvisation, Walking Bass Lines and Chord Melody." It sold well in the Ann Arbor Michigan area for a number of years, then after a while people stopped purchasing it. I stopped promoting it and put it on the shelf and sat there for about three years. Then it dawned on me that there was nothing wrong with the video, I just needed to reach a wider audience. I sent a copy to three publishers that I thought would be interested in the product. I figured that I would start at the top so I contacted three of the most prominent publishers of music instructional material. I contacted: Mel Bay publications, Hal Leonard publications and a third company whose name I forget. I put together a letter of introduction, which explained who I was and what I had to offer and what I wanted them to do. I mailed the letters along with a copy of my instructional videotape and eagerly awaited a response.

The first response came from the company whose name I cannot remember. I think

I have forgotten their name because, they sent my video back to me along with a rejection letter that stated; they did not publish the band material. That rejection did not bother me because it was obvious that they did not even watch the video. They just responded with a form rejection letter that had no bearing on my guitar playing or my product. The video featured me playing solo guitar. At least they returned my videotape.

The second response came from Hal Leonard. They were very professional with a rejection letter, which read; thank you for submitting your instructional videotape. You are an excellent guitarist however; we already have a product that covers the information that you covered in your video. Good luck with your future endeavors. They too returned my videotape.

Hal Leonard's response was both encouraging and discouraging at the same time. Encouraging because they let me know that I was on to something but discouraging because in my opinion they were the second largest publisher and they turned me down.

I thought surely that Mel Bay, the largest publisher would have a video that covers the information that was covered in my video. I had given up on hearing from Mel Bay publications after three or four months had passed.

One day I was giving guitar lessons and the phone kept on ringing, interrupting the lessons. The phone calls had literally interrupted all of the lessons that I had that day. I was giving lessons of the last event for the day. This father stayed inside my house to read while I gave his son his guitar lesson. After about 10 minutes into the lesson the phone rang again. I asked the student's father, if he would mind answering the phone and taking a message for me. He answered and said to me; John you might want to take this call because it is from the president of Mel Bay publications. I agreed and took the call.

When I answered, the voice on the other hand said: "John, my name is William Bay, I am the president of Mel Bay Publications. I apologize for taking so long to get back in touch with you but, my father Mel Bay recently passed, and I had to take care of a lot of things." I told him not a problem, I understand after all that is your father.

He told me that he liked my instructional video and he thought that I was an excellent guitarist and that he would like to publish it. He went on to say that he did not have any books in their catalog that covers the material the way that I did in the video. He said he not only wanted to publish the video that he wanted me to write three books based on the concepts that was covered in the video and he would published them as well. William Bay the president of Mel Bay publications said that he would draft a letter outlining what we had discussed over the phone and he would send it to me along with the publishing contracts. Look them over and take it to your attorney, feel free to make any changes that you feel are necessary signed them 'and send them back to me and we will go from there. I thanked him and hung up the phone. I was so excited that I could hardly finish the guitar lesson.

It took me about eleven months but, I finished the books and they are now being sold worldwide. There are multiple lessons to be learned from this story they are:

- If your product has sold well in your area, then that is a good indication that it will sell in other parts of the world. Expand your customer base.

- Do not be afraid to start at the top when you are searching for company to work with.

- Believe in yourself and your product.

- Do not give up.

The following are examples of the books that I wrote for Mel Bay Publications. I have included a book description along to give you an idea of the content of the books.

Business Management for the Working Musician

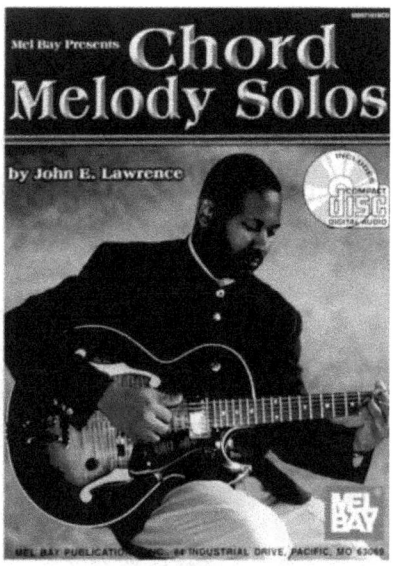

The exercises and tunes in this book involve playing the chords and the melody of a song simultaneously. This book outlines six basic steps for playing guitar effectively in the chord melody style. Chord reference diagrams in major, minor, and dominant categories are provided to expand your harmonic palette. The book's exercises will acquaint you with this popular style and assist you in developing the requisite techniques. Written in standard notation and tablature 48 pages.

John E. Lawrence

This book presents step-by-step instruction on how to build an improvised guitar solo in four stages: Motive, Development, Climax, and Closing Gesture. The book also includes five types of solos: swing, funk, ballad, blues, and Latin. These last five solos are in the form of songs to give players a more realistic sense of how improvisation works. Written in standard notation and tablature with chord grids.

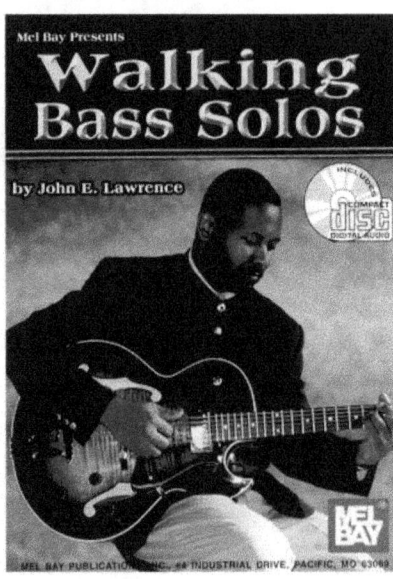

This book teaches guitarists how to play chords and bass lines simultaneously while providing insight to bass line construction. Includes exercises to enhance the playing of chord changes and bass lines, plus bass solos that illustrate specific styles including walking blues, jazz swing, and bossa nova. Exercises include: Constructing Walking Bass Solos Root - 5th; Root - 5th - Leading Tone; What Is a -V-I Chord Progression; The Major Walk; Root - 5th and Octave; Slow Blues Line; 12-Bar Blues Progression No. 1; 12-Bar Blues Progression No. 2; 12-Bar Blues Progression No. 3; Putting It All Together; and New Bossa - 40 pages written in notation and tablature.

Shortly after the completion of my books I received another letter from the president of Mel Bay publications William Bay. He informed me that Mel Bay Publications was embarking on a new business venture. They wanted to publish a book that would feature songs complete with solo by sixty of the world's best guitarists. The book will be entitled The Master Anthology of Jazz Guitar Solos. He wanted to know if I would be interested in contributing a song to be featured in the book. I thought about it for moment I said to myself, they are considering me as one of the best guitarist in the world. Needless to say, I said yes.

John E. Lawrence

Business Management for the Working Musician

The completion of the Mel Bay books triggered a chain of events that led me to other business opportunities that took my career to a new level. For instance; a friend of mine by the name of Joe Sussane asked my permission to contact some guitar manufacturing companies to see if he could get me an endorsement deal with them. I said, "Let's go for it." He contacted two companies initially: Gibson Guitars and Heritage Guitars. The representative for Gibson Guitars told us that Gibson does not give out endorsement deals because; they want the workmanship and the quality of the instrument to speak for itself.

The representative at Heritage Guitars was very receptive to the idea of offering me an endorsement deal. I spoke with William Bay that Mel Bay publications and explained to him that I was working on getting an endorsement deal with Heritage Guitar Company. I asked him would it be possible to take a picture of me holding a Heritage guitar and use it for the front cover of my books. We agree and that clinched the endorsement deal with Heritage guitars.

Heritage guitar Company was formed when Gibson Guitar Company left Kalamazoo Michigan. Some of the workers at Gibson stayed at the old Gibson factory and started Heritage Guitars. In my opinion, Heritage makes their instruments with the same craftsmanship as Gibson because the same people that may Gibson guitars are now making Heritage guitars. Some aspects of the Heritage guitars are better than Gibson guitars because we have to go the extra mile to be competitive with Gibson. Heritage is more creative when it comes to the finishes the colors and styles of the guitars and in my opinion their trademark is the creative design and finish of the pick guard. They built with the same quality as a Gibson, but they have a more affordable price.

After I signed the endorsement contract with Heritage Guitars, Bill Paige informed me that every guitar that leaves the heritage guitar factory is strung with GHS Guitar strings. He said now that I am one of their artists I could probably get an endorsement deal with GHS Guitar Strings. Bill Paige gave me a person's name and contact information at GHS guitars strings and said that he would contact him first and tell them about me, so he would be expecting my call. When I contacted the GHS Guitar Strings they knew who I was, and they welcomed me with open arms.

I endorsed GHS guitar strings for about three or four years, the top of endorsement deal allowed me to purchase guitar strings at two dollars per set, which is about 60% off the retail price. Then one day I received a letter from Mel Bay publications informing of a new promotional campaign between Mel Bay and LaBella guitar strings. Mel Bay would print with pictures of selected Mel Bay authors and their books along with the author's bio. The inserts will be placed into every set of LaBella guitar strings and circulated worldwide. In return, the authors would receive free guitar strings and LaBella will get Mel Bay's authors to endorse their strings.

My relationship with GHS guitar strings was a good one and I did not want to leave them but the deal with LaBella was too good to pass up. I would receive free advertising and free guitar strings, so I called the GHS and explained the offer that I had received LaBella. I told them that I would no longer be endorsing GHS strings. He understood and wished me the best. They told me that if things did not work out with LaBella that I am always welcome to come back to GHS.

Next, we set out to get an endorsement deal with acoustic guitar manufacturers. I ended up signing with Takamine Guitars. I like the style and feel of their guitars, and I particularly enjoy the electronics Takamine puts into their high-end acoustic guitars. Their bridge mounted pick-ups are able to amplify all of the subtle nuances that I add to my music as well as the percussive sounds I generate when I play the guitar. They were the first guitar company that I know of to have a built-in guitar tuner, nine presets and digital reverb built into the electronics of the guitar.

CHAPTER 14

TURNING POINTS IN MY LIFE

Someone asked me the question: "How did you become successful in life?" I have to say that it was a combination of things that has made my life what it is today. First, there was a love of music that dates back as far as I can remember. Then there was a love for the guitar that began when I was nine years old. The love of the guitar was so strong that I would practice every day for hours at a time. Even 46 years later, I still manage to fit in about eight hours of practice a day. I could not have done it without the support that was given to me from my parents, my family and my community.

As I look back on my life, I can now see some decisions that I made took me in a direction that led me to where I am today. I did not realize it at the time, but there are some events that happened and if I had turned right instead of left, my life could have taken me in a totally different direction.

Turning Point I

One day my fourth-grade teacher asked all of the students to display their talent in front of the class. One of my classmates by the name of Michael Lewis played his guitar for the class and I was so impressed with his playing that I asked him to teach me how to play. He said yes, and I followed him to his house after school. He taught me my first two songs, which were "Louie Louie" and a song entitled, "Twine Time." Those songs began my love affair with the guitar.

That experience could have gone a totally different way. What if Michael had said "No, I will not teach you?" Michael could have chosen to keep his talent to himself, but instead he decided to share it with me. I have been playing the guitar ever since. Michael Lewis actually stepped into my life and changed it forever.

John E. Lawrence

A SUPPORT SYSTEM AND THE IMPORTANCE OF POSITIVE REINFORCEMENT

It is important to surround yourself with people that believe in you and what you are trying to accomplish. One negative comment can have more of an impact on a person than fifty positive reinforcements.

There was an experiment conducted at the Summer Institute for talented and gifted high school students in the Arts and Sciences. The institute was held on the campus of Eastern Michigan University in Ypsilanti Michigan.

One student was asked to stand in the front of the room and people lined up to say something positive and nice about the student. People said things like:

- You are very intelligent
- You are a joy to be around you have a very pleasant personality
- I believe in you and I know you will achieve all of the goals in life
- I am glad that I have met you because you have proven yourself to be a true friend
- I aspire to be like you, you are a fine example of a human being

Imagine forty-five more people giving such comments to this person and then the last person in the line told the student something like, "You will never amount to anything, I think you are the stupidest person in the program and I wish that I had never met you."

Which comment do you think would have the most impact on the student? Which one would they remember for the rest of their life?

If your answer is the negative comment, then you are correct. This is why it is so important to surround yourself with positive people and to make a conscious effort to stay away from negative people. Negative people will cause you to have self-doubt, which can prevent you from trying to achieve your goals.

I have been very fortunate to have people in my life that believed in me. Without the support and guidance from some key people in my life, I do not think that I would be where I am today.

I joined my first band when I was at the age twelve. We would rehearse Monday through Thursday in the basement of my parent's house. During those days, we would practice at a loud volume, but my parents never complained. We kept this practice schedule from when I was in the seventh grade through high school. The band became very popular where we performed every weekend.

My father is a master carpenter, electrician and mechanic. He is one of the smartest men I that have ever known. He built my first guitar amplifier and first PA system for the band. He even became the band's manager. My father helped the band buy a bus so that we could travel to performances together. My father did all this while working two jobs to support a family of five children and a wife. This is where I got my work ethic from.

My mother would be upstairs in the kitchen cooking for the family while the band would be downstairs rehearsing. She was the one that had to put up with all of the loud music and loud talking for all those years.

My mother has always given me encouragement and still today, she is my biggest fan. She still continues to come to my performances to show support, forty years later.

I would like to take this opportunity to thank my parents, Hugh and Marjorie Lawrence, for their unending support, love, and guidance that has made me the man I am today.

Even my grandmother was supportive. I can still hear her say as I sat practicing my guitar, "He's going to be somebody someday."

Turning Point II

I did not realize it at the time but, the biggest risk that I ever took in my life ended up being a turning point in my career.

When I was about twenty-three years old I worked in an automobile factory. Back then, jobs were easy to find, and the pay was good. Most of the people that worked in the auto industry usually stayed there until retirement. However, that was not the case for me. After my 90-day trial period I thought to myself, I am all set to have this job for life. I recall thinking to myself this is easy, I can do this!

All I have to do is go to work every day and pay my bills. I went to work six days a week, twelve hours a day for one year. That was my routine. I did not practice my guitar because, by the time I got off work I didn't have the energy to play. One day it dawned on me, either I was going to be a factory worker or a musician. I couldn't do both. I had worked that job for exactly one year and the next day I quit, and I never looked back.

Turning Point III

Leaving the factory marked a turning point in my life because that is when I was first introduced to Dr. Morris J. Lawrence Jr., the founder and Department Chair of the Washtenaw Community College Performing Arts Department. Two female singers from my first band told me about this great college professor at WCC. They said you have to meet him!

When I met Morris, I had my guitar and a drawing of Bruce Lee that I had made. He asked to play for him and afterwards he complemented by playing and said that he liked my phrasing. I did not know what he meant by phrasing because, I was self-taught and had no formal training. I figured it must mean something good, so I smiled and said thank you.

He went on to say that I was pretty good but, it is still a lot for me to learn. Dr. Lawrence told me to start coming to his classes and learn much from him as possible.

Dr. Morris Lawrence was a great teacher and he was the first teacher that I ever had that made it enjoyable to learn. I was thirsty for his knowledge and I came to every class that he taught which consisted of:

- The Washtenaw Community College Jazz Orchestra
- Jazz Combo
- Songwriting
- Music Appreciation and Music Theory
- Afromusicology

Afromusicology is a phrase coined by Dr. Lawrence, which is the study of American musical characteristics from an Afrocentric perspective.

I attended WCC four days a week for years learning as much as I could from Dr. Lawrence. He taught me the art of jazz improvisation, which teaches how to structure a solo in a way that tells a musical story that has a beginning, middle and an end. I learned how to be more expressive when I played music. Through his tutelage, I learned things like music composition and how to arrange different instruments. Dr. Lawrence always said that I should give 110% every time I play my guitar.

Dr. Morris Lawrence is the reason why I am instructor at Washtenaw Community College today. He saw the natural teaching ability in me before I did. Morris offered me my first teaching position at WCC 30 years ago. Initially I said no because, I did not think that I could handle the job but, he insisted, so I acted upon his faith in me and accept the job. It turns out that he was right; I love teaching. It comes natural to me and I think that I am pretty good at it.

John E. Lawrence

Dr. Morris J. Lawrence passed away in 1994 and I now hold the same position he had at WCC. It is now my turn to carry on where he left off.

CHAPTER 15

PERSONAL GROWTH

I tell my guitar students that I am teaching from experience. There are things that I have worked on for long periods of time and have made a noticeable difference in my playing style and growth as a guitarist. On the other hand, there are things that I have worked on for long periods of time that have not made a noticeable difference; in fact, they actually hindered my growth as a guitarist. I call them stumbling blocks or road blocks. My job as an instructor is to teach students in a way that will maximize their efforts and navigate them around any road blocks, thereby supplying them with a more direct path to success. This book is designed to the same thing as it pertains to building a musical career. The purpose of writing this book is to help navigate musicians through the stumbling blocks or roadblocks of life.

This book is based on the ideas and choices that have taught me valuable lessons in my lifetime. The lessons have enabled me to develop and grow as a musician, a businessman and as an individual. These ideas and choices have led me to where I am in life today. I am still learning, growing and developing and in no way do I consider myself finished. I still have goals and dreams that I have yet to accomplish and once I have attained these goals and dreams, my plan is to create new ones and continue this cycle.

In order for me to be honest and fair, I must admit that not every choice that I made has worked out for my betterment. Someone once said that "we are the sum of the choices we have made in our lives". Therefore, we must take responsibility for where we are in life.

A wrong choice I made was to put my career before my son. I thought in order to be a successful musician I had to be totally committed to the music. I did not balance time between my career and my son properly. I defined success as being the best guitarist in the world. My goal was to be the best, or at least, I would be one of the best. There is a saying that goes "Shoot for the moon and if you don't make it, at least you will land among the stars." But no one ever talks about the level of commitment and sacrifice it takes to really shoot for the moon.

After my son became an adult, he told that he felt that he came second to my music. He came second to my practice time, second to my performances, second to my recording sessions and second to my songwriting. He was right! Now that I am older and wiser, I know that if I had spent more time with my son, I would still be an excellent guitarist and just as far along in my career.

Business Management for the Working Musician

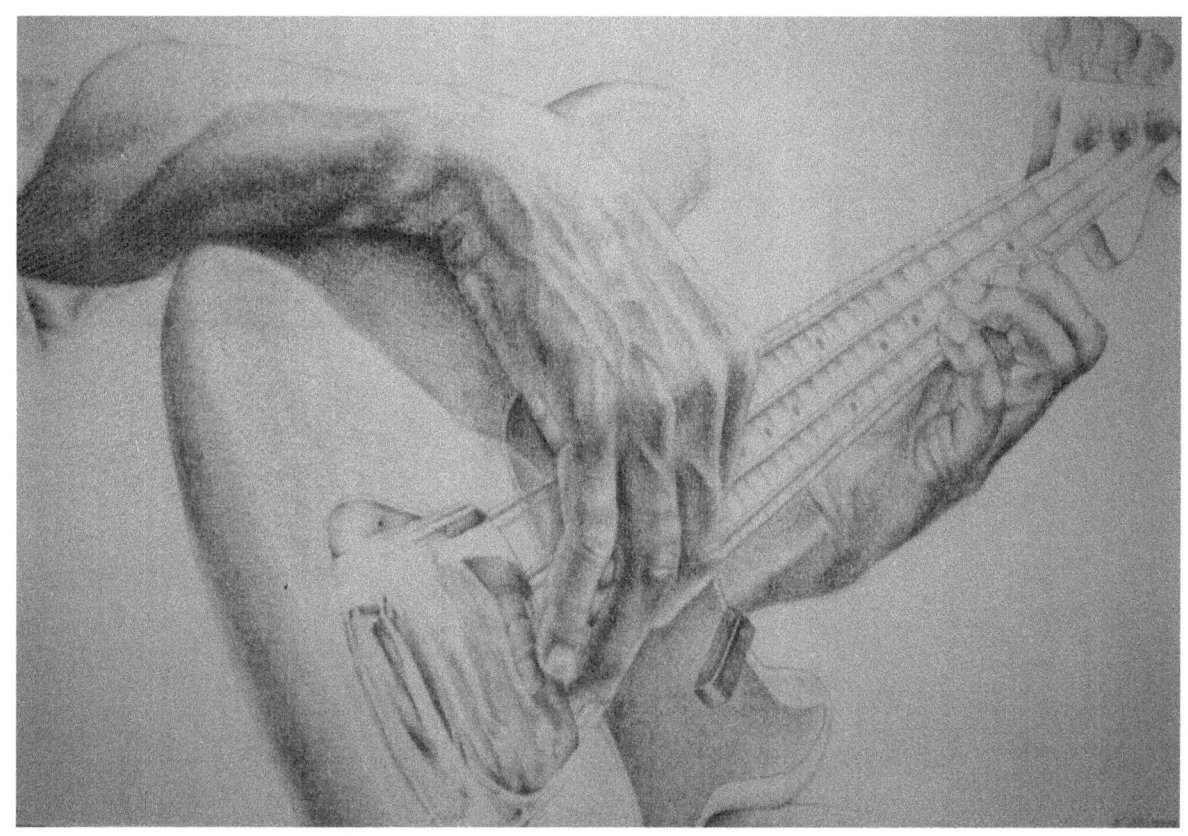

Artwork by John E. Lawrence

John E. Lawrence

www.ingramcontent.com/pod-product-compliance
Lightning Source LLC
Chambersburg PA
CBHW080509110426
42742CB00017B/3044